Jatia Cookbook

Elaine Hallgarten

A MARTIN BOOK

Published by Martin Books
an imprint of Woodhead-Faulkner Ltd
Fitzwilliam House, 32 Trumpington Street, Cambridge CB2 1QY
in association with the Citrus Marketing Board of Israel
Market Towers, Nine Elms Lane, London SW8 5NX

First published 1984
© The Citrus Marketing Board of Israel and Elaine Hallgarten
1984
ISBN 0 85941 278 4

Design: Ken Vail Graphic Design
Photography: John Lee
Food preparation for photography: Ann Page-Wood
Typesetting: Hands Fotoset, Leicester
Printed in Great Britain by Springbourne Press Limited,
Basildon, Essex

Contents

Introduction 5

Breakfast
Grilled Jaffa Grapefruit 14
Grilled Bacon and Grapefruit 14
Grapefruit Baskets 14
Jaffa Salads 15
Yogurt and Citrus 15
Porridge Topped with Citrus 15
Jaffa Omelette 15
Breakfast in a Glass 15

Soups and Hors d'Oeuvres
Salade Tiède 16
Tomato Orange Mould 18
Ceviche 18
Grapefruit and Pernod Sorbet 19
Pickled Herring and Kumquat Salad 20
Cucumber Cheese Mould 22
Pink Grapefruit and Cardamom 22
Grapefruit and Smoked Mackerel 23
Curried Avocado and Citrus Salad 24
Pomelo and Prawns 24
Jaffa Grapefruit and Ginger Soup 26
Iced Prawn and Yogurt Soup 27

Avocado and Lime Soup 27
Cocktail Titbits 28
Egg and Lemon Soup 28
Grapefruit and Pasta Salad 30

Main Courses
Beef and Kumquat Salad 32
Coriander and Orange Pork 34
Spiced Beef Casserole 35
Gammon and Grapefruit 35
Roast Duck Taruschio 36
Chicken Livers in Orange Sauce 38
Piquant Chicken 39
Jaffa Kebabs 39
Turkey Fillets with Grapefruit and Cumin 40
Turkey and Pomelo Salad 40
Slimmers' Salad 42
Veal in Jaffa Cream Sauce 43
Honey-glazed Chicken 43
Fish with Orange Mustard Sauce 44
Liver and Lime 46
Paprika Lamb 46
Grilled Lemon Chicken 47
Sole with Pink Grapefruit and Fennel 48

Sauces
Cumberland Sauce 50
Egg and Lemon Sauce 51
Sweet Jaffa Sauce 51

Cranberry and Orange Sauce
52
Kumquat Purée   53
Jaffa French Dressing   53

Salads and Vegetables
Carrot and Orange Salad   54
Spinach and Orange Salad   55
Carrot Purée with Lime   55
Caraway Cabbage and Lemon
56
Green Beans in Orange Sauce
56
Coleslaw with Easy Peelers
58
Avocado and Grapefruit Salad
58
Red Cabbage and Grapefruit
58
Spiced Parsnips with Orange
59
Marrow with Dill and Lime
59
Minted Jaffa Red Blush and
Chinese Leaves   60
Orange, Onion and Olive Salad
60
Jaffa Fennel Salad   60

Desserts
Syllabub   62
Gin and Lime Posset   63
Lemon Roulade   64
Sorbets   66–67
Citrus Strudel   67
Sunrise Special   68

Flambéed Pomelo   68
St Clement's Soufflé   70
Lemon Meringue Pie   71
Jaffa Trifle   72
Candied Kumquats   72
Sweet Jaffa Salads   74–75
Orange Soured Cream Cake
76
Orange Cream   78
Jaffa Valentine   79
Jaffa Gratin   80
Sussex Pond Pudding   81
Lemon Mousse   82
Frozen Jaffa Cream   83
Orange Chocolate Frosting
84
Lemon Icing   84

Preserves and Drinks
Marmalade   85–87
Fruit Curds   87–88
Spiced Oranges or Kumquats
88
Candied Peel   90
Jaffa Chutney   91
Lemonade   92
Real Planter's Punch   92
Buck's Fizz   92
Nimboo Pan   94
Citron Pressé   94
Classic Cocktails with Jaffa
94–95
Jaffa Mull   95
Trio   96

Introduction

'Oranges and lemons, say the bells of St Clement's'. This familiar nursery song, written in the mid-eighteenth century, celebrates fruits which are now a familiar feature of our everyday lives. Over the years many other members of the Jaffa family have become welcome additions to our fruit bowls, and every year they appear in time to brighten our winter gloom, bringing a touch of Israeli sunshine.

Most citrus fruit seems to have originated in or around north-west India, though there are claims of its provenance from other parts of Asia. The word 'orange' may well have derived from the sanskrit *nagaranga*. However, the fruit may possibly have been introduced to India from China during the first centuries.

The fruits were brought to Europe by Arab traders and later by the Crusaders, who discovered oranges in Palestine, now Israel. They were cultivated in Spain and Italy and later France, where Royalty planted orange trees in their ornamental gardens and protected them in winter by constructing immense glasshouses, or orangeries. Oranges were served at a Royal banquet in England in 1399 and by the mid-sixteenth century were already being used in cooking, according to a cookery book dating from 1539. Nell Gwyn certainly helped to popularise oranges — an early example perhaps of a successful Public Relations exercise! Oranges were 'cried' on the streets of London in the seventeenth century, and recipes using both oranges and lemons are frequently found in books from that time onwards. A typical dish was *Salmogondy*, which included orange and lemon.

Cultivation of limes was introduced to the West Indies by the British, who had long realised the nutritional benefits of citrus fruit in combating scurvy, a hazard of long sea journeys. The British Navy issued rations of lemon juice, and later lime juice, spiked with rum, thus creating the nickname 'limeys', which to this day many North Americans fondly call their British cousins.

Today, a wide range of Jaffa citrus fruit is grown in, and exported from, Israel. The many varieties have all found their way into my kitchen and my cooking pots, because, as cooks through the ages have found, the flavour-enhancing properties of citrus fruit make them a most useful companion to almost any food. The nutritional properties of citrus fruit also play an important role in a healthy diet. I have thoroughly enjoyed developing recipes with all the beautiful Jaffa fruit, and I hope you will find, as you use this book, that these delicious and nutritious fruits can sparkle throughout the meal — not just, as might be thought, at breakfast or for dessert, but with fish and meat and with savoury and sweet dishes.

Meet the Jaffa family of citrus fruit

Grapefruit: There are different varieties of grapefruit, depending on the time of year, the earliest being the *Yarden River,* from November, which grows in the Jordan Valley. This is followed by the regular and the spring grapefruit. All 'white' grapefruit derive from the white marsh variety. The 'red' grapefruit are developed from different botanical varieties: *Red Blush* from the Ruby Red and *Sunrise* from the Star Ruby. The vividness of colour and succulence of these really beautiful fruits make them particularly attractive for cooking. *Sunrise* is most aptly named — truly reminiscent of a Mediterranean sunrise!

Oranges: There are three main varieties of Jaffa oranges. *Navels* — easily recognised by their round shape and distinctive 'navel' on the underside; *Shamouti* — with their typical oval shape, easier to peel than the Navel; and the *Valencia Lates* — round and very juicy with thin, smooth skin.

Lemons: These are available all the year round and are an indispensable ingredient in any cooking, helping to heighten flavours, keeping food from discolouring, and invaluable as a natural diuretic and in medications. They are also used in cosmetics. Lemons are high in pectin and are often included in jam recipes to help in the setting.

Limes: These arrive in the summer and are a close cousin of the lemon. They are in fact sometimes known as green lemons. The juice is very acid and is much used in mixed drinks. The flavour is distinctively different from the lemon, but you could, generally speaking, substitute lemons for limes in many recipes.

Easy peelers: When I was young, there were tangerines, and that was that. Now we have a whole range of soft citrus fruit which goes by the descriptive name of 'easy peeler'. Easy peelers are invariably hybrids of different fruits, and the main ones from Jaffa are the **mineola,** a cross between a tangerine and grapefruit, with a vivid orange-coloured bell shape and few pips; the **temple,** which is a hybrid of a mandarin and an orange, with a rich, spicy flavour; and **topaz,** which is a mixture of an orange and a tangerine, and arrives from Spring onwards, when there is no other soft citrus on the market. Collectively these fruits are known as **Jaffarines** and are all exceptionally juicy. You might see various other varieties from time to time, as Jaffa are constantly experimenting with new strains.

Pomelo: This is the largest of all the citrus fruits and has the thickest peel. (Never throw the peel away — it makes marvellous candied peel or marmalade.) It is sometimes known as **Shaddock,** after the English sea captain who originally brought it from Polynesia to Jamaica. It is now cultivated in Israel, where early records show that it was found in the twelfth century. The pulp of the fruit is virtually sealed in by its thick membrane. It is almost crisp in texture, and is sweet to eat.

Kumquats: These are the smallest citrus fruit, with a thin, sweet skin and a tart-flavoured flesh. The name derives from the Cantonese *Kam Kwat*. The whole of the fruit is edible, and makes a pretty garnish to many different dishes, either glistening in a light syrup, or eaten raw for an interesting, bitter-sweet taste.

Preparing Jaffa citrus fruit

Every citrus fruit consists of peel, pith, membranes, flesh and pips, to a greater or lesser degree. In this book I use the word 'peel' when it includes the pith and 'rind' when all the pith is removed. The outermost part of the rind is the zest, which contains essential oils and a great deal of flavour. The flesh, which is covered with membranes which divide it into segments, consists of tiny droplet-like particles called vesicles.

To segment oranges and grapefruit (and also lemons and limes, although they are not often segmented), remove the peel and pith completely, using a very sharp knife. First cut off a slice from the top of the fruit. Stand the fruit upright on a flat surface and, following the shape of the fruit, cut away the peel and pith right round the fruit. Cut off the bottom piece of the peel and trim away any pith still remaining. Using a sharp, pointed knife, and holding the fruit over a bowl to catch any juice, cut carefully between the membranes to loosen the flesh and gently ease it away.

Jaffa's pomelos can be peeled in the same way, but the membrane is particularly stiff and can be peeled away by hand to loosen the flesh.

Easy peelers have much softer flesh, which tends to fall apart if the membrane is removed. It is better just gently to scrape away any pith and then break the fruit into segments with the membrane attached, or, if needed for garnish, carefully slice each segment lengthways and use with the flesh side up, membrane side down.

To make grapefruit (or orange) baskets, draw a line around the fruit with a pencil, about two thirds of the way up. Mark a handle across the top and then cut the peel away from the sides of the handle. Cut out the flesh from the rest of the fruit, using a grapefruit knife if possible.

To make orange or lemon shells for filling, just cut off the top of the fruit and scoop out the flesh with a grapefruit knife, finishing with a teaspoon. Fill with sorbet or, as a pretty garnish, fill with peas, tiny carrots or fish mayonnaise.

To make matchsticks (or julienne strips), use a sharp potato peeler to cut away strips from oranges or lemons and lay these on a board. Cut into even thinner strips, using a sharp knife, and use as required — if possible, blanch the rind before use. To blanch rind, cover with boiling water and cook for about 5 minutes. Drain.

To caramelise rind, make a sugar syrup with 175 ml/6 fl oz water and 175 g/6 oz sugar. Add the blanched matchsticks to this syrup and cook until the syrup begins to caramelise, about 15 minutes. Use as decoration or make caramel oranges with orange slices.

To make poached orange (or lemon) slices, make a syrup as for caramelised rind, above. Thinly slice the oranges, with the peel on, and cook them in the syrup until the peel begins to soften. Remove from the heat before the slices lose their shape. Use as a decoration.

To grate rind/zest, use a sharp grater or, better still, a citrus zester, which is a very useful tool. Always grate fruit before cutting, if possible. To obtain the flavour of the essential oils, rub the zest of the fruit with sugar lumps whenever sugar is needed in the recipe.

Grapefruit Baskets (page 14); Porridge Topped with Citrus (page 15)

To make lemon (or lime, or orange) twists, cut a thin slice of the fruit and then make a cut half-way across, from the edge to the centre. Twist each half gently in an opposite direction.

Cut lemons, limes and oranges into wedges (with the peel on), for decorating and squeezing over fish, etc.

Use a cannelling knife to make ridges in oranges or lemons before slicing, for a pretty effect, or to make strips of peel for decorations.

To squeeze any citrus fruit, lemons and limes in particular, roll the fruit on a hard surface first. This helps to soften the fruit and makes it easier to extract the juice.

Buying and storing Jaffa fruit

A general rule of thumb is that the heavier the fruit, the juicier it will be, so when buying citrus, choose the heaviest and firmest fruit you can find. When the fruit is young and healthy, its condition is reflected in its skin, which should be shiny, firm and rich in colour. This shine decreases with age and the skin loosens — much as it does with humans! Large, soft spots are a sign of bruising.

Citrus fruit is best stored in a cold shed or a really cool pantry. Central heating wreaks havoc with all fruit and refrigerating citrus is not advised, as it dries the skin. You can wrap the fruit in cling film to keep it even longer. Slices of lemon or lime, open-frozen and then stored in a container, are useful for garnishing and for drinks — alcoholic or otherwise. Juice frozen in ice cube trays is a handy way to keep a ready supply for cooking purposes. Lemon and orange shells, well wrapped, are always useful when you need the odd piece of rind for flavouring soups and sauces. Try keeping a good supply of grated zest in the freezer, in a well sealed container.

C — for citrus and vitamin!

The nutritional aspect of citrus fruit is extremely important, especially in the winter months. All varieties contain large amounts of Vitamin C, indeed, they are the most reliable source of this vitamin. The protective skin of the fruit prevents loss of Vitamin C in transit and in storage, and when the fruits are eaten raw there is no loss of vitamin. Cooking the fruit does, sadly, diminish the nutritional value. A medium-size Jaffa orange contains approximately 86 mg of Vitamin C, which is more than double your daily nutritional requirement. Oranges are also rich in potassium and calcium. A grapefruit has about 74 mg of Vitamin C. Vitamin C helps prevent bleeding gums and sore mouths. Pregnant women and young children need extra amounts, but even so, an orange (or grapefruit) a day fulfils all their needs. In addition to 96 mg of Vitamin C, lemons also contain Vitamins A and B. All citrus fruits contain fibre.

Slimming — Jaffa style

Citrus fruits are always high on any slimmer's diet sheet. They are high in water content and have a correspondingly low energy content, their energy coming from carbohydrate (fructose and glucose), with very little protein and salt, and no fat. A medium-size orange has about 60 kilocalories; a white grapefruit has 43; a red grapefruit 51. A lemon has a mere 18 kilocalories and an easy peeler about 20.

Beauty and the citrus

Freshly squeezed lemon juice is useful for removing stains, for instance, on cigarette-stained fingers or work-grimed hands. Save the squeezed halves of lemons and rub them into your hands before washing. Use a cotton bud soaked in freshly squeezed lemon juice for stubborn stains under and down the sides of nails.

Make a bleaching pack for hands — mix freshly squeezed lemon juice with corn oil, cover your hands with this mixture and allow to soak in. Cream your hands thoroughly and then rinse off.

To make a honey and lemon face mask for normal skin, combine 15 ml spoon (1 tablespoon) slightly warmed honey with 5 ml spoon (1 teaspoon) freshly squeezed lemon juice. Blend together, then apply to the face. Leave for 30 minutes before washing off.

A tip for removing freckles is found in Mrs Beeton's Book of Household Management: mix 25 ml (1 fl oz) Jamaica rum with 25 ml (1 fl oz) each of vinegar and rose water. Add 75 ml (3 fl oz) freshly squeezed lemon juice. This lotion should be applied to freckles freely during the day, with a soft linen handkerchief, after which the affected parts should be lightly powdered.

For a lemon juice hair rinse, make a mixture with 600 ml (1 pint) water and 60 ml (2½ fl oz) freshly squeezed lemon juice. Use to rinse the hair, to make it shiny. To lighten hair, use a stronger solution: 600 ml (1 pint) water and 150 ml (¼ pint) lemon juice.

To soften hard skin on your feet and elbows, rub with lemon halves. Add grapefruit juice to your bath for a refreshing skin tonic.

And, as an aid to household beauty, rub a lemon half over your chopping board to clean away onion and other smells. Add lemon juice to salt for cleaning copper pans, and use lemon juice to take out stains in clothes (but test for colour fastness first).

Cultivating citrus

For no cost at all you can start your own citrus grove — well, a mini grove, which may not actually produce fruit but which will give you some pretty green foliage. Simply push any pips into a pot of soil and put in a warm sunny spot (my kitchen window-sill has proved ideal). Keep it well watered. Be patient and, after some weeks or possibly months, you will have the beginnings of your grove. Transplant to individual pots to grow stronger plants.

Make a Jaffa pomander

An old-fashioned, clove-studded orange is lovely to hang in a cupboard. Take a firm-skinned orange and press in cloves to cover it completely. Thread a silk ribbon round it and leave in your wardrobe to perfume your clothes. This makes a lovely gift, too. To make a potable pomander, use only 12 cloves to each orange and place in a jar or bottle. Cover with 100 g (4 oz) sugar and a bottle of gin. Shake from time to time until the sugar is dissolved and then leave for 3 months. Strain the liquid and keep in a clean bottle. Drink as required!

Note: In this book both metric and imperial measures are given. Use either one or the other, but do not mix them. All recipes serve 4 unless otherwise stated.

Acknowledgements:

My most sincere thanks to the many friends who have generously given me recipes, and to my family, who ate their way through all the recipes — both the failures and the successes — with equanimity and only the odd groan.

Grilled Jaffa Grapefruit with different toppings (page 14)

Breakfast

I wouldn't mind betting that most people, if asked with which meal they associated a grapefruit, or indeed any citrus fruit, would automatically answer 'breakfast'. I hope, in the rest of this book, to prove that citrus fruit can be used happily throughout the meal and throughout the day, but for the sake of brightening up your breakfast table, here are some ideas to wake you up.

Grilled Jaffa Grapefruit
(Pictured on page 13)
Prepare half a grapefruit by cutting through the segments and loosening all the flesh really well (there's nothing so infuriating as having to struggle with a stubborn piece of grapefruit first thing in the morning). Use a grapefruit knife for this if possible.

Spread your chosen topping over the grapefruit and grill it for at least 5 minutes, to make sure it gets warmed right through. Reduce the heat of the grill if it begins to burn.

Toppings: Try any of the following: a spoonful of any marmalade; a spoonful of peach, apricot or blackcurrant jam; cinnamon sugar; honey mixed with breadcrumbs.

Grilled Bacon and Grapefruit
Wrap a piece of streaky bacon around a segment of grapefruit (or half a segment if they are large). Secure the bacon with a cocktail stick. Grill until the bacon is crisp.

Grapefruit Baskets
(Pictured on page 9)
Although this is a fiddly thing to do first thing in the morning, it makes a pretty start to anyone's day (and you can always prepare the baskets the day before). Follow the instructions on page 8 for making a citrus basket, removing the flesh carefully with a grapefruit knife. Zig-zag the edges for extra effect. Dice the flesh and return it to the basket. You could mix the flesh with other

fruit, such as kiwifruit (which always look dramatic) or just the odd cherry. Serve cold.

Jaffa Salads

See the dessert section for a few ideas on citrus salads — any combination of citrus fruits makes a refreshing salad, suitable for breakfast or any other meal.

Yogurt and Citrus

Cut up the segments of a grapefruit, an orange or an easy peeler and mix with natural yogurt. Serve with or without a sprinkling of sugar, as desired.

Porridge Topped with Citrus

(Pictured on page 9)

Cook your porridge according to the instructions on the packet and pour into a bowl. Carefully lay segments of grapefruit or orange on top. Serve as it is or sprinkle a little brown sugar over the fruit and then pop under a grill just to melt the sugar — a delicious, nutritious and filling way to go off to school or work!

Jaffa Omelette

Make an omelette and fill with a spoonful of chopped citrus fruit or marmalade, for an unusual taste sensation.

Breakfast in a Glass

Makes 1 tall glass

	juice of ½ grapefruit or 1 orange	
150 ml	natural yogurt	¼ pint
5 ml spoon	clear honey	1 teaspoon
1	egg	1

Combine all the ingredients together in a blender and mix for several minutes. Pour into a tall glass and drink immediately.

Use Sunrise or Red Blush grapefruit for a delicious pink tinge. Omit the egg, if you like, for a less rich drink.

Soups and Hors d'Oeuvres

The first course can set the tone for the meal, titillating the taste buds. Whether you make a big production out of it, or it is just a gentle hint of things to come, the addition of a little citrus will certainly provide an appetising beginning.

For instant success: serve chilled Jaffa grapefruit in halves (with all the segments separated and the flesh well loosened), with a shot of spirit poured on top – try gin, kümmel, Pernod or crème de cassis.

Add freshly squeezed orange juice to canned tomato soup (hot or cold), with a blob of soured cream and some finely grated rind.

Add freshly squeezed lemon juice to canned consommé, with a twist of lemon to decorate.

Salade Tiède

One of the nouvelle cuisine ideas which greatly appeals to me is that of serving a small but attractive salad topped with a morsel of warm meat, fish, or, as in this case, delicate chicken livers.

1	heart of curly endive	1
6	radicchio leaves	6
2	oranges, segmented	2
225 g	chicken livers	8 oz
25 g	butter	1 oz
15 ml spoon	brandy	1 tablespoon
3 x 15 ml spoon	french dressing (made with lemon)	3 tablespoons
	salt and pepper	

Cover the centre of four medium-size plates with a small salad, consisting of some pieces of the endive, carefully trimmed and cut into small fronds, and the radicchio, torn into small pieces. Arrange the orange segments in a ring on top of each salad.

Wash the livers and pat them dry. Remove any green bile. Melt

Tomato Orange Mould; Salade Tiède

the butter and cook the livers very quickly – they should still be pink in the middle. Add the brandy and seasoning and stir the livers round well. Spoon the dressing over each plate just to moisten the salad lightly. Place a quarter of the livers in the centre of each plate. Serve immediately.

Tomato Orange Mould

397 g	can of tomatoes	14 oz
3	spring onions, chopped	3
150 ml	natural yogurt or soured cream	¼ pint
2	oranges, grated rind of 1 and juice of 2	2
1½ x 15 ml spoon	gelatine	1½ tablespoons
200 ml	strong beef stock	7 fl oz
	salt and pepper	

Put the tomatoes in a large bowl and break them up a little with a fork. Add the chopped spring onions, yogurt or soured cream and the grated orange rind. Pour the orange juice into another bowl and sprinkle on the gelatine. Leave to soak for 5 minutes. Heat the stock, add the orange and gelatine and stir until dissolved. Cool and then stir into the tomato mixture, amalgamating well. Check the seasoning.

Rinse a mould with cold water and then spoon the mixture into the mould. Refrigerate until set – preferably overnight. Unmould and serve with some watercress or crisp salad leaves.

Ceviche

Raw fish isn't to everyone's taste, but this dish from Mexico (via Jaffa!) is something special. The lime juice in which the fish is marinated has the effect of cooking it.

450 g	haddock or halibut, filleted and diced	1 lb
75 ml	lime juice	3 fl oz
225 g	tomatoes, peeled and seeded	8 oz
1	green pepper, diced	1
4 x 15 ml spoon	olive oil	4 tablespoons
15 ml spoon	white wine vinegar	1 tablespoon
15 ml spoon	chopped fresh oregano	1 tablespoon
2 x 15 ml spoon	chopped parsley	2 tablespoons
	a dash of tabasco sauce	
	salt and pepper	
	lettuce leaves, to garnish (optional)	

Put the diced fish in a glass bowl and pour on the lime juice. Marinate for 3 hours, covered, in the refrigerator. Then chop the tomatoes and add to the fish, together with all the remaining ingredients except for the lettuce leaves. Mix carefully and refrigerate until required.

Either serve from the bowl or make individual portions by lining four small dishes with lettuce and then spooning the fish into the dishes.

This dish can also be served as a main course with salads.

Grapefruit and Pernod Sorbet

This never fails to please, and is a really appetising starter. Substitute gin or kümmel for the Pernod if you aren't sure that everyone likes the taste of aniseed.

75 g	sugar	3 oz
150 ml	water	¼ pint
2	large grapefruit, segmented	2
3 x 15 ml spoon	Pernod	3 tablespoons
1	egg white	1

Dissolve the sugar in the water and simmer for 5 minutes to make a syrup. Leave to cool. Cut the grapefruit segments in half, removing any pips. Place the fruit and the syrup in a blender and liquidise. Pour into a plastic container and, when it is cool, stir in the

Pernod. Cover and place in the freezer for a minimum of 8 hours, or overnight.

When the mixture has frozen solid, remove it from the freezer. Beat the egg white until stiff. Place the mixture in a blender or food processor and mix to soften, then fold in the stiffly beaten egg white, mixing until light and smooth. Return to the freezer for a further 6 hours, or more if possible.

A short time before you want to serve the sorbet, place four glasses in the freezer to chill. Make balls of sorbet and place them on a plate in the freezer. Just before serving, put a ball of sorbet into each glass and serve immediately – it melts very quickly.

Decorate with a twist of grapefruit peel or a sprig of fennel.

Pickled Herring and Kumquat Salad

You may think this is a bizarre combination of flavours, but it actually works well and looks extremely pretty.

75 g	sugar	3 oz
300 ml	water	½ pint
16	kumquats	16
approx. 450 g	jar of pickled herrings with onions	approx. 1 lb
3 x 15 ml spoon	soured cream	3 tablespoons
	endive or crisp lettuce leaves, shredded	

Dissolve the sugar in the water. Add the kumquats and poach them gently for 10 minutes only. (Put a plate on the kumquats while they are cooking, to keep them under the liquid.) Drain and cool the kumquats as soon as they are cooked (use the liquid for a fruit salad).

Drain the liquid from the jar of herrings. Cut the herrings and onions into thin slices. Mix with the soured cream. Put a layer of endive or shredded lettuce on to four plates. Garnish each one with 4 kumquats. Refrigerate and serve well chilled.

Cucumber Cheese Mould; Pickled Herring and Kumquat Salad

Cucumber Cheese Mould

142 g	packet of lime jelly	5 oz
75 ml	boiling water	3 fl oz
75 ml	lime juice	3 fl oz
175 g	curd cheese	6 oz
3 x 15 ml spoon	corn oil	3 tablespoons
2 x 15 ml spoon	white wine vinegar	2 tablespoons
15 ml spoon	horseradish cream	1 tablespoon
2	spring onions, chopped	2
1	medium-size cucumber	1
5 ml spoon	salt	1 teaspoon
	pepper	

Put the jelly in a small saucepan and pour on the boiling water. Stir over a very low heat to dissolve the jelly and pour it into a large bowl. Add the lime juice, curd cheese, oil, vinegar, horseradish and spring onion. Beat well until the mixture is smooth. Then refrigerate until it is partially set.

Meanwhile, cut 12 thin slices from the cucumber and reserve them for decoration. Grate the cucumber into a bowl and add the salt. When the jelly is beginning to set, drain the cucumber and add it to the jelly, mixing well. Add pepper to taste. Rinse a small mould with cold water, then spoon the cucumber mixture into it. Refrigerate until set. Unmould and decorate with the cucumber slices. Serve as a first course or as a salad with cold meat or chicken.

Pink Grapefruit and Cardamom

The rich succulence of Jaffa Red Blush or Sunrise Grapefruit are enhanced by the delicacy of this subtly spicy sauce.

3 x 15 ml spoon	clear honey	3 tablespoons
2 x 15 ml spoon	water	2 tablespoons
2	cardamom pods	2
75 ml	fruity white wine	3 fl oz
2	Red Blush or Sunrise grapefruit, segmented	2

Put the honey and water in a saucepan. Remove and crush the seeds from the cardamom pods and add to the pan. Bring to the boil, then reduce the heat and simmer for 5 minutes. Add the wine and leave to cool.

Cut the grapefruit segments in half if they are very thick, discarding any pips. Put the fruit in a bowl and pour over the cooled liquid. Refrigerate until required and serve very cold.

You can use ordinary grapefruit for this, in which case try a rosé wine, which gives it a little colour.

Grapefruit and Smoked Mackerel

Grapefruit goes well with fish, especially smoked, and this is the sort of useful dish you can easily make from ingredients you are likely to have in the house. Frozen smoked mackerel fillets are excellent to have as a standby and they defrost quite quickly.

2	grapefruit, segmented	2
approx. 275 g	smoked mackerel fillets	approx. 10 oz
2 x 15 ml spoon	horseradish cream	2 tablespoons
2 x 15 ml spoon	soured or whipped cream	2 tablespoons
	paprika	
	lettuce leaves, to garnish (optional)	

Drain the grapefruit segments and cut them in half. Put in a bowl. Remove the skin from the mackerel and flake the flesh into the bowl. Mix the horseradish cream and soured or whipped cream together and pour on to the grapefruit and mackerel. Mix gently.

To serve, you can either put the mixture in a serving dish, garnished with lettuce leaves, or you can serve the mixture in the grapefruit shells, or in small glasses. Sprinkle paprika over the top and refrigerate until required.

Curried Avocado and Citrus Salad

Any combination of citrus and avocado is good, but here I use pomelo to give a crisp texture and mineola for its wonderful juiciness.

½	pomelo, segmented	½
2	mineolas	2
3 x 15 ml spoon	mayonnaise	3 tablespoons
15 ml spoon	yogurt	1 tablespoon
15 ml spoon	chutney	1 tablespoon
5 ml spoon	curry powder	1 teaspoon
1	large avocado	1

Cut each segment of the pomelo into 2 or 3 pieces. Put in a large bowl. Segment 1 mineola and cut each segment in half. Add to the bowl. Mix the mayonnaise, yogurt, chutney and curry powder together thoroughly and add to the bowl. Refrigerate until required.

Just before serving, cut up the avocado and gently mix it into the contents of the bowl. Spoon into four glasses or small dishes. Peel the second mineola and remove as much pith as possible. Cut each segment in half through the middle, taking care not to break the membrane. Decorate each salad with the mineola segments, cut-side up to show the colour.

Pomelo and Prawns

This is a variation of an old favourite of grapefruit and prawns. The crispness of the pomelo makes a nice change, and you can use the peel to make an attractive serving dish.

1	pomelo	1
175 g	peeled prawns	6 oz
4 x 15 ml spoon	mayonnaise	4 tablespoons
15 ml spoon	soured cream or natural yogurt	1 tablespoon
	˜a dash of tabasco sauce	

Pomelo and Prawns; Curried Avocado and Citrus Salad

Cut the pomelo into quarters and, with a sharp knife, carefully take the fruit off the peel, keeping the peel intact so that you have a boat-shaped container for the salad. Remove all the pith and the membrane from the fruit, and put the flesh in a bowl. If there are any large pieces, cut them up. Add the prawns. Mix the mayonnaise, soured cream or yogurt and tabasco together and pour over the pomelo and prawns. Mix well. Spoon the mixture on to the four 'boats' and refrigerate until required.

For a change, substitute canned tuna for the prawns. You can use 2 grapefruit instead of the pomelo, if preferred. Wipe the pomelo skins after use and make candied peel with them (page 90).

Jaffa Grapefruit and Ginger Soup

Cold fruit soups are popular in many European countries, and are lovely on a hot summer's evening (or in a centrally heated house!). This one is pale and interesting, and is really a cross between a soup and a drink. Serve in bowls or glasses, as you like.

300 ml	white wine	½ pint
600 ml	water	1 pint
3 x 15 ml spoon	sugar	3 tablespoons
2	large grapefruit	2
1	piece of stem ginger, chopped finely	1
2 x 15 ml spoon	cornflour	2 tablespoons
3 x 15 ml spoon	water	3 tablespoons
300 ml	natural yogurt	½ pint

Put the wine, the 600 ml (1 pint) water and the sugar in a large pan. Cut off two slivers of grapefruit rind and add to the pan. Finely grate the rind of the other grapefruit and reserve it, in a closed container. Now peel both grapefruit, removing all the pith. Cut into chunks and discard the pips. Add to the pan with the ginger and heat gently. Mix the cornflour with the 3 x 15 ml spoon (3 tablespoons) water and add to the pan, stirring well. Bring to the boil and then simmer gently for 20 minutes.

Cool the soup and then blend in a food processor or blender with the yogurt. Refrigerate until required and serve very cold, garnished with the reserved grapefruit rind.

Iced Prawn and Yogurt Soup

This is really half-way between a soup and a hors d'oeuvre, since there isn't a great deal of liquid in it. However, that which we call a soup tastes just as good by any other name! Serve it in small bowls.

175 g	prawns, defrosted if frozen	6 oz
450 ml	natural yogurt	¾ pint
2	large oranges, juice of	2
2	spring onions, chopped	2
2 x 15 ml spoon	soured or whipped cream	2 tablespoons
	salt and pepper	

Reserve 12 prawns and chop up the remainder. Put the chopped prawns in a large bowl and add the yogurt, orange juice and chopped spring onions. Add salt and pepper and mix well. Refrigerate until required.

Spoon into four small bowls and put a blob of the soured or whipped cream on top of each. Garnish with the reserved prawns.

Avocado and Lime Soup

2	limes	2
2	medium-size avocados	2
900 ml	cold chicken stock	1½ pints
150 ml	single cream	¼ pint
	salt and pepper	

Cut the limes in half and then cut off one thin slice from each half. Reserve these slices and squeeze the juice from the limes. Cut the avocados in half and put the flesh in a blender or food processor. Add the lime juice, stock and cream. Blend until smooth. Taste and add salt and pepper as required.

Refrigerate the soup until required and then spoon into four bowls. Garnish each bowl with the reserved lime slices.

Cocktail Titbits

You can always conjure up something to go with a drink if you have some Jaffa fruit and a fridge full of odds and ends. Mix and match whatever you have to hand.

Segment a grapefruit and cut each segment in half, or into thirds if large. Wrap strips of smoked salmon or Parma ham around each piece and secure with a cocktail stick.

Cut thick chunks of salami and spear with a cocktail stick. Add half a segment of orange.

Break easy peelers into segments (keeping the membrane intact) and wrap around with thin strips of soft garlic sausage or mortadella. Secure with a cocktail stick.

Cut bite-size pieces of herring pickled in spices or wine and spear on a cocktail stick with a piece of orange, easy peeler or half a candied kumquat.

Chop orange segments and mix into curd cheese. Add a little chopped stem ginger. Spread on to bite-size pieces of pumpernickel bread or crackers, or use as a dip with celery or green pepper sticks.

Egg and Lemon Soup

There are many versions of this delicate soup, the most famous being Greek *Avgolemono*. Mine is a Polish variation, since I prefer a little sugar to offset the sharpness of the lemon.

110 ml	lemon juice	4 fl oz
5 ml spoon	sugar	1 teaspoon
2 x 15 ml spoon	long grain rice	2 tablespoons
1 litre	chicken stock	1¾ pints
4	egg yolks	4
	salt and pepper	

Add the lemon juice, sugar and rice to the chicken stock and put in a large pan. Bring to the boil. Beat the egg yolks, and, when the soup is boiling, add half to the beaten yolks, a drop at a time,

Cocktail Titbits

beating continually. When half the hot liquid has been added to the yolks, return the mixture to the pan on a very low heat – do not boil or the eggs will curdle. Just heat through, very gently. Correct the seasoning before serving.

Note: To make an unusual cold soup, make the soup as above, but omit the rice. Soak 2 x 15 ml spoon (2 tablespoons) gelatine with 4 x 15 ml spoon (4 tablespoons) water for 5 minutes. Stir into the hot soup. Mix until the gelatine has dissolved. This makes enough for six, so pour into glasses or bowls and leave to set. Cover each bowl of jellied soup with a thin layer of soured cream, and top with chopped chives.

Grapefruit and Pasta Salad

This substantial first course would also make a good supper dish or part of a buffet.

2	grapefruit, segmented	2
100 g	salami or ham	4 oz
1	large pickled cucumber	1
2 x 15 ml spoon	mayonnaise	2 tablespoons
15 ml spoon	Dijon mustard	1 tablespoon
100 g	pasta, cooked	4 oz
	lettuce, shredded, to garnish (optional)	

Cut the grapefruit segments in half and put in a bowl. Cut the salami or ham into strips and the cucumber into dice and add both to the grapefruit. Mix the mayonnaise and mustard together and pour on to the grapefruit mixture. Add the cold pasta and mix everything together well.

Serve in small bowls on a bed of shredded lettuce, or in grapefruit shells.

Main Courses

In this chapter you will find a wide variety of dishes, from the quickly made to the more elaborate. Citrus can give a lift to quite ordinary everyday foods – here are eleven quick tips to tempt you.

Add freshly squeezed lemon juice and a little grated rind to stock or water when cooking rice, or add to cooked rice with some butter.

Add freshly squeezed orange juice to the pan juices of grilled lamb chops (after skimming off excess fat), heat through and pour over the meat.

For a sauce for fish, add orange juice to the pan after sautéeing the fish in butter. Garnish with orange segments.

Use freshly squeezed lemon juice as a tenderiser for meat and poultry: mix 110 ml (4 fl oz) olive oil with half that amount of lemon juice, plus garlic, salt and pepper. Add some fresh herbs and marinate meat or poultry in the mixture for a few hours. Grill.

Make your favourite chicken salad with an orange mayonnaise and serve in hollowed-out orange shells (chill the shells before use).

Cold duck with oranges, green peppers and green olives, bound together with orange mayonnaise, makes an unusual salad.

Cold turkey fillets dressed with lemon mayonnaise makes an easy meal.

Serve cold fish salad or just cold poached salmon with orange mayonnaise, garnished with orange slices.

Grill pork or lamb chops with a coat of kumquat purée (page 53).

Try egg and lemon sauce with fish, poultry or meat – a blissful companion for anything (page 51).

Gremolata is a mixture of chopped parsley, garlic and finely grated orange and lemon rind, usually added to *Osso Buco Milanese,* but there's nothing to stop you adding it to any meat dish – veal, beef or poultry – to give it extra zing.

Beef and Kumquat Salad

My friend Aileen, who created this dish, modestly refers to it as a 'buffet dish of ineffable elegance'. I agree with her — it's a show stopper. Though it appears to be complicated, much of it can be prepared in advance and then put together at the last minute. There are three main parts: the beef, the sauce, and the kumquats and vegetables.

Tail end of fillet, which is much cheaper than whole fillet, is quite suitable for this. All the Chinese ingredients for the sauce are available in specialist Chinese shops and some supermarkets. Cold rice, cooked in beef stock, makes a good accompaniment.

450 g	beef fillet	1 lb
2 x 15 ml spoon	oil	2 tablespoons
	For the sauce:	
2 x 15 ml spoon	hoi sin sauce	2 tablespoons
3 x 15 ml spoon	soya sauce	3 tablespoons
15 ml spoon	dark muscovado sugar	1 tablespoon
5 ml spoon	chopped fresh ginger root	1 teaspoon
1	large clove of garlic, crushed	1
15 ml spoon	sesame oil	1 tablespoon
	For the vegetables:	
175 g	kumquats	6 oz
75 g	sugar	3 oz
300 ml	water	½ pint
1	green pepper, with the seeds removed	1
8	spring onions, trimmed	8
100 g	mange tout, trimmed	4 oz
15 cm piece	cucumber, peeled	6-inch piece
225 g	fresh bean sprouts	8 oz

Cut the beef fillet into slices, 4 cm (1½ inches) thick. Mix all the sauce ingredients together and pour on to the beef slices. Mix well and leave to marinate, overnight if possible, but for at least 6 hours.

Poach the kumquats in the sugar and water for 10 minutes only

(put a plate on the kumquats while they are cooking, to keep them under the liquid). Remove from the liquid as soon as they are cooked, and leave to cool. Cut the pepper into strips about 5 mm (¼ inch) thick, cut the spring onions into strips, then cut the cucumber into strips of about 5 mm (¼ inch). Put the bean sprouts on to a large dish. Blanch all the other vegetables separately, just long enough to soften them slightly – they should be 'al dente'. Keep them in separate piles as you drain each vegetable.

A few hours before you want to serve the dish, remove the meat from the sauce (reserve the sauce) and pat it dry. Heat the oil and fry the meat for about 3 minutes on each side, until it is lightly cooked. Remove from the heat and slice into strips. (The meat should be quite rare on the inside.) Leave to cool. Reserve half of each of the blanched vegetables and the poached kumquats for garnish. Halve the remaining kumquats and gently mix with the rest of the vegetables and the meat, together with the reserved sauce. Place the vegetable and meat mixture on top of the bed of bean sprouts. Decorate with all the reserved vegetables and whole kumquats. Serve cold.

Coriander and Orange Pork

Coriander seems to have a special affinity with orange and both go well with pork.

575 g	pork fillet, sliced thinly	1¼ lb
	seasoned flour	
40 g	butter	1½ oz
15 ml spoon	ground coriander	1 tablespoon
3	oranges, juice of	3
2 x 15 ml spoon	orange marmalade	2 tablespoons

Pass the sliced pork through the flour. Heat the butter, add the pork and cook for a few minutes on each side before adding the coriander. Stir round well. Add the orange juice, cover and cook on a low heat for about 15 minutes, until the pork is cooked through. Remove the meat from the pan, stir in the marmalade and heat through. Spoon the sauce over the meat and serve immediately.

Spiced Beef Casserole

800 g	stewing beef, cubed	1¾ lb
3 x 15 ml spoon	seasoned flour	3 tablespoons
	oil	
225 g	onions, sliced	8 oz
100 g	carrots, sliced	4 oz
15 ml spoon	curry powder	1 tablespoon
450 ml	beef stock	¾ pint
3	oranges, juice of 2 and whole segments of 1	3

Pass the beef through the seasoned flour. In a casserole, heat the oil
and soften the sliced onion in it. Add the carrot and stir round for a
few minutes. Remove the onion and carrot from the pan. Add a
little more oil and then the prepared beef, a few pieces at a time,
browning well. When all the meat is browned, return the onion
and carrot to the casserole. Add the curry powder and stir well.
Add the stock and the orange juice. Bring to the boil, cover and
cook in the oven at 150°C/300°F/Gas Mark 2 for 2½ hours.

Just before serving, add the orange segments, halved.

Gammon and Grapefruit

1.4 kg	corner cut of gammon	3 lb
2 x 15 ml spoon	dark muscovado sugar	2 tablespoons
15 ml spoon	Dijon mustard	1 tablespoon
2	grapefruit, segmented	2

Cover the gammon with water and boil for 1½ hours. Remove
from the pan and carefully take off the rind. Mix the sugar and
mustard together and spread over the gammon. Place the gammon
in a roasting tin and add the grapefruit segments. Bake at
200°C/400°F/Gas Mark 6 for 20 minutes.

Roast Duck Taruschio

I made the acquaintance of this dish at The Walnut Tree Inn near Abergavenny – perhaps an unlikely place to find an Italian, Franco Taruschio, producing sensational food. He very kindly sent me this recipe. He uses mallard, but duck will do as well – it is the sauce that makes it so very special.

2.2–2.25 kg	duck	4½–5 lb
1	small onion, chopped finely	1
1	small carrot, chopped finely	1
15 ml spoon	butter	1 tablespoon
3	tomatoes, chopped	3
15 ml spoon	plain flour	1 tablespoon
450 ml	veal stock (or use a stock cube and water)	¾ pint
1	bouquet garni	1
175 g	sugar	6 oz
150 ml	white wine vinegar	¼ pint
20	kumquats	20
2 x 15 ml spoon	Grand Marnier	2 tablespoons
	salt and pepper	
	watercress, to garnish	

Season the duck, prick it all over and roast at 190°C/375°F/Gas Mark 5 for 1½–2 hours. Meanwhile, make the sauce. Soften the chopped onion and carrot in the butter. Add the chopped tomatoes and cook for a few minutes. Add the flour and stir well. Cook for 2 minutes. Add the stock and the bouquet garni. Simmer for 30 minutes, skimming regularly.

In another saucepan, melt the sugar very slowly until it begins to take on a little colour. Add the vinegar and stir over a low heat – the sugar may go hard, but keep stirring and it will melt again. Strain the sauce on to this mixture and cook for a further 10 minutes. Add the kumquats and cook very gently for 10 minutes more.

When the duck is ready, remove from the oven and cut into serving pieces. Put on to a large dish. Sprinkle with the Grand

Roast Duck Taruschio

Marnier and spoon over the sauce with the kumquats. Garnish with the watercress. Serve immediately with any extra sauce in a sauceboat.

This sauce is also good with chicken. If you cannot find a large duck, use 2 smaller ones.

Chicken Livers in Orange Sauce

Calorie counters will be pleased to have this recipe, which tastes great but only clocks up 215 calories per serving.

575 g	chicken livers	1¼ lb
175 ml	tomato juice	6 fl oz
3	oranges, juice of 2 and segments of 1	3
5 ml spoon	finely chopped fresh ginger root	1 teaspoon
1	large green pepper, with the seeds removed and cut into strips	1
2	sticks of celery, chopped	2
4	spring onions, trimmed and cut into strips	4
	salt and pepper	

Wash the chicken livers, removing any bits of green bile. Pat them dry and put in a flameproof, shallow dish. Season with salt and pepper. Place the dish under the grill and cook the livers for about 8–10 minutes, turning them to cook on all sides.

While they are grilling, put the tomato juice in a saucepan and add the orange juice, ginger, salt and pepper. Heat through gently. Add the green pepper, celery and spring onion and let them cook in the sauce for 2–3 minutes, just to soften slightly.

When the livers are ready, spoon the sauce and vegetables over them. Garnish with the segments of orange and serve immediately.

Piquant Chicken

1.6–1.8 kg	chicken, cut into 4	3½–4 lb
110 ml	oil	4 fl oz
110 ml	lime juice	4 fl oz
1	small onion	1
2.5 ml spoon	tabasco sauce	½ teaspoon
2.5 ml spoon	salt	½ teaspoon
2 x 15 ml spoon	tomato ketchup	2 tablespoons

Place the quartered chicken in a shallow ovenproof dish. Put the remaining ingredients in a blender and mix until smooth. Pour over the chicken and leave to marinate for 2 hours. Cook in the oven at 190°C/375°F/Gas Mark 5 for 45 minutes.

If preferred, you can barbecue the chicken, basting with the sauce.

Jaffa Kebabs

50 ml	lime juice	2 fl oz
1	medium-size onion, grated	1
2 x 15 ml spoon	olive oil	2 tablespoons
15 ml spoon	curry powder	1 tablespoon
2 x 5 ml spoon	ground turmeric	2 teaspoons
2 x 5 ml spoon	ground ginger	2 teaspoons
a pinch	chilli powder	a pinch
1	large clove of garlic, crushed	1
700 g	boneless lamb, cubed	1½ lb
1	lime, quartered	1

Blend together all the ingredients except the lamb and the quartered lime. Put the lamb in a shallow dish and pour over the blended ingredients. Leave to marinate for a minimum of 3 hours.

Thread the pieces of lamb on to skewers and grill under a hot grill (or over a barbecue if preferred), basting with the marinade.

Serve with the lime quarters.

Turkey Fillets with Grapefruit and Cumin

Turkey fillets are a most useful standby — their blandness·is a
virtue, an empty canvas on which to paint your own picture.

2 x 15 ml spoon	oil	2 tablespoons
700 g	turkey fillets	1½ lb
2 x 5 ml spoon	ground cumin	2 teaspoons
2 x 15 ml spoon	plain flour	2 tablespoons
2	grapefruit, juice and pulp of	2
3 x 15 ml spoon	sweet (single) or soured cream	3 tablespoons
	salt and pepper	

Heat the oil and add the turkey fillets. Brown well on each side.
Add the cumin and stir well. Remove the turkey. Add the flour,
stirring well. Add the grapefruit juice and pulp. Cook, stirring
continually, to make a smooth sauce. Return the turkey to the pan
and cook on a low heat, covered, until the turkey is done — about 10
minutes. Stir in the cream and salt and pepper just before serving.

Turkey and Pomelo Salad

By good chance, cold turkey and pomelo happened to be around at
the same time, so this salad resulted!

450 g	cooked turkey, diced	1 lb
1	pomelo, segmented and cut into chunks	1
3	sticks of celery, chopped	3
2	large tomatoes, cut into chunks	2
1	large green pepper, with the seeds removed and chopped	1
110 ml	mayonnaise	4 fl oz
75 ml	natural yogurt	3 fl oz
5 ml spoon	curry powder	1 teaspoon

In a large bowl, combine the turkey with the pomelo, celery,
tomato and green pepper. Mix the mayonnaise with the yogurt and

Turkey and Pomelo Salad; Slimmers' Salad

curry powder. Add to the turkey and mix thoroughly. Refrigerate until required. Serve on a bed of crispy salad if liked.

You could use cooked chicken for a change or substitute 225 g (8 oz) ham for half of the turkey. Try adding hard-boiled eggs to the dish.

Slimmers' Salad

Anyone who has been on a diet will have attempted to make cottage cheese just a little more interesting. Citrus fruit really does help to liven up the blandness and make it look more attractive, and this version is most appetising.

	crisp lettuce, endive and chicory leaves	
450 g	plain cottage cheese	1 lb
½	pomelo, segmented	½
1	orange, segmented	1
1	grapefruit, segmented	1
1	mineola or topaz, segmented	1
1	green pepper, with the seeds removed and cut into strips	1
½	small fennel, cut into strips	½
4	small button mushrooms	4
	french dressing or lemon juice	

Make a bed of the crisp leaves on four plates. Put a quarter of the cottage cheese on to the centre of each plate. Cut the pomelo segments in half. Cover the cottage cheese with alternate strips of the fruits. Place the green pepper and fennel around the edge and put a button mushroom in the centre of each. Serve the french dressing or lemon juice separately.

Veal in Jaffa Cream Sauce

	seasoned flour	
575 g	veal escalope	1¼ lb
25 g	butter	1 oz
15 ml spoon	oil	1 tablespoon
225 ml	orange juice	8 fl oz
75 ml	lemon juice	3 fl oz
3 x 15 ml spoon	double cream	3 tablespoons
	grated rind of 1 orange, cut into matchsticks and blanched (page 8)	

Lightly flour the veal. Heat the butter and oil together and fry the veal for about 3 minutes on each side, depending on the thickness. Remove from the pan and keep warm. Add the orange and lemon juice and bring to the boil, stirring well to scrape the sediment from the bottom of the pan. Reduce the heat, add the cream and stir round. Spoon the sauce over the veal and sprinkle with the prepared orange rind before serving.

Honey-glazed Chicken

1.6–1.8 kg	chicken	3½–4 lb
2	small grapefruit, juice of	2
3 x 2.5 ml spoon	ground ginger	1½ teaspoons
3 x 2.5 ml spoon	ground cinnamon	1½ teaspoons
4 x 15 ml spoon	honey	4 tablespoons

Place the chicken in a roasting tin. Mix the remaining ingredients together and pour over the chicken. Cook for 1 hour in the oven at 190°C/375°F/Gas Mark 5, basting frequently with the sauce. Remove the chicken from the pan and keep warm. Carefully remove as much fat as possible. Heat the juices in the pan, adding a little boiling water if the sauce is very thick.

Carve the chicken and spoon over the sauce.

Fish with Orange Mustard Sauce

You can use this marvellous sauce for any fish you fancy (it is so good, I would even eat it on stale bread!). Salmon and haddock are just two alternatives to those given here.

4, approx. 225 g each	mackerel or trout, cleaned and skinned, with the heads left on	4, approx. 8 oz each
1	lemon, juice of	1
50 g	butter	2 oz
2	oranges, grated rind of 1 and juice of 2	2
15 ml spoon	Dijon mustard	1 tablespoon
2 x 15 ml spoon	chopped parsley	2 tablespoons
1	egg yolk	1
	salt and pepper	

Place the fish in a greased, shallow oven dish. Season well and pour on the juice of the lemon. Cover and bake in the oven at 180°C/350°F/Gas Mark 4 for about 30 minutes.

While the fish is cooking, make the sauce. Melt the butter, taking care not to burn it. Add the grated rind of 1 orange and the juice of both, whisking into the butter. Add the mustard and the parsley. Simmer for 2 minutes.

Stir the egg yolk in a small bowl and drop the hot sauce in very slowly, beating all the time. Return the sauce to the pan and cook on the lowest possible heat to thicken a little. Do not boil. Keep hot in a pan of water if necessary, until required.

When the fish is cooked, remove from the oven and carefully lift on to a warm serving dish. Spoon over some of the sauce and serve the rest separately. (You may prefer to remove the skin of the fish after cooking, before spooning on the sauce.)

Liver and Lime

Calf's liver is my favourite, but use ox or lamb's liver if preferred.

450 g	liver, sliced thinly	1 lb
	seasoned flour	
3 x 15 ml spoon	oil	3 tablespoons
2 x 15 ml spoon	butter	2 tablespoons
110 ml	lime juice	4 fl oz
	grated lime rind	
397 g	canned artichoke hearts, drained and quartered	14 oz

Pass the slices of liver through the seasoned flour. Heat the oil and butter together and fry the liver for just a few minutes on each side. Don't overcook it – it should still be pink in the middle. Remove the liver and keep warm. Add the lime juice and grated rind to the pan, together with the artichoke hearts. Heat through, stirring to scrape the sediment from the bottom of the pan. Spoon the sauce and artichoke hearts over the liver and serve immediately. Garnish with extra slices of lime if you like.

Paprika Lamb

Shoulder of lamb is good for this dish, but remove any excess fat.

15 ml spoon	oil	1 tablespoon
700 g	boneless lamb, cubed	1½ lb
1	large onion, sliced	1
2 x 15 ml spoon	paprika	2 tablespoons
2	lemons, juice of	2
3 x 15 ml spoon	chopped parsley	3 tablespoons
110 ml	water	4 fl oz
	salt and pepper	
	soured cream, to garnish (optional)	

Heat the oil and brown the meat in it. Remove from the pan and add the onion. Cook until softened, then add the paprika, lemon juice and parsley. Add salt and pepper and mix everything well. Return the meat to the pan and add the water. Cook, covered, on a very low heat until the meat is tender, about 40 minutes.

Serve with a dollop of soured cream on top if liked.

Grilled Lemon Chicken

1.6–1.8 kg	chicken, cut into 8 pieces	3½–4 lb
200 ml	lemon juice	7 fl oz
50 ml	olive oil	2 fl oz
2	large cloves of garlic, crushed	2
a pinch	ground cloves	a pinch
a pinch	ground cinnamon	a pinch
	salt and pepper	
1	lemon, quartered, for garnish	1

Place the chicken in a large shallow dish. Mix the lemon juice, oil, garlic, salt and pepper together well. Rub the ground spices into the chicken. Pour the lemon juice mixture over the chicken, rubbing it in well. Leave to marinate overnight, turning the pieces from time to time.

Heat the grill and brush the wire tray with oil. Grill the chicken until cooked through thoroughly. The skin should be crisp and you must take care that the meat is cooked right through to the bone. Brush with the marinade frequently. Serve hot, with the quartered lemon.

This is even better cooked on a barbecue, and eaten with your fingers.

Sole with Pink Grapefruit and Fennel

The beautiful Red Blush or Sunrise grapefruit is shown off to perfection in this recipe – it makes a stunning colour contrast to the white of the fish and the green of the fennel, and has an unusual taste.

60 g	butter	2½ oz
approx. 700 g	lemon sole fillets	approx. 1½ lb
450 g	fennel, with plenty of green fern	1 lb
40 g	plain flour	1½ oz
600 ml	milk	1 pint
1	Sunrise or Red Blush grapefruit, segmented	1
	salt and pepper	

Cut up 15 g (½ oz) of the butter into small pieces and dot on to each fish fillet. Remove the fern from the fennel and chop it up finely. Sprinkle a little on to each fillet. Season well and roll up the fillets, placing them in a lightly greased oven dish. Bake at 180°C/ 350°F/Gas Mark 4 for 25 minutes.

Thinly slice the fennel and cook in boiling salted water for about 4 minutes – don't overcook it; it should still have a little bite. Drain and reserve.

Make a white sauce: melt the remaining butter, add the flour and mix in well. Slowly add the milk, stirring continually and cook until thickened. Season generously. Add the cooked fennel and keep warm on a very low heat.

Cut each grapefruit segment in half lengthways. When the fish is cooked, remove the dish from the oven, spoon over the fennel sauce and arrange the grapefruit segments around the top. Serve immediately.

You can use plaice or sole for this dish if preferred – you will need either 12 medium-size or 8 large fillets.

Sole with Pink Grapefruit and Fennel

Sauces

Sauces and citrus fruit have quite a lot in common, with their ability to complement food. A sauce can add just that extra something to give a plain dish style and finish, and that's exactly what citrus flavours do, lifting and enhancing the taste of savoury and sweet dishes. So put a dash of Jaffa into your sauce and the result is bound to be great.

Just a sliver of lemon or orange rind is a *sine qua non* of home-made tomato sauce, and a grating of rind can lift even a commercial sauce. Use a squeeze of lemon juice to rescue an over-sweet sauce (whether home-made or bottled).

When you make mayonnaise, substitute citrus juice for vinegar, which gives you a more delicate flavour. Lemon juice goes with everything, but try orange or lime for a change.

Cumberland Sauce

This is a classic British sauce, used with cold poultry or ham. I use it also for lamb and roast duck.

1	large orange	1
½	lemon	½
100 g	redcurrant jelly	4 oz
2.5 ml spoon	dry mustard	½ teaspoon
75 ml	red wine	3 fl oz

Remove the rind from the orange, cut into matchsticks and blanch (see page 8). Squeeze the juice from the orange and the lemon and pour into a saucepan, together with the remaining ingredients. Bring to the boil, stirring to dissolve the jelly. Cook for 2 minutes, add the blanched orange rind and leave to cool. Serve cold.

Egg and Lemon Sauce

Apart from being a great favourite of mine, this sauce is most versatile, suitable for almost any vegetable, meat, fish or poultry. Adapt it as necessary, using the liquid from your cooking or adding stock to make up the liquid.

75 ml	lemon juice	3 fl oz
300 ml	stock or liquid from cooked vegetables, fish or poultry	½ pint
a pinch	sugar (optional)	a pinch
3	egg yolks	3
	salt and pepper	

Add the lemon juice to the stock, with the sugar, if used. Beat well and then drop the hot liquid on to the yolks in a bowl, very slowly, beating constantly. Return the mixture to the saucepan on a very low heat and warm through gently, stirring constantly. Do not boil. Taste and correct the seasoning, adding a little more sugar if necessary. Pour over the vegetables or meat, and serve.

Sweet Jaffa Sauce

Having made this sauce to go with pancakes, I thought it was too good to use just for one dessert and tried it over cooked pasta, to make an amazing pudding. Try it over ice cream – stunning! Even better, cook some vol-au-vent pastry cases, pop a scoop of ice cream in each and top with the hot sauce.

20 g	butter	¾ oz
100 g	sugar	4 oz
3	large oranges	3
1	large lemon	1
3 x 15 ml spoon	brandy (optional)	3 tablespoons

Melt the butter in a large frying pan and add the sugar, stirring until it begins to dissolve. Keep the heat low, otherwise the sugar will caramelise. Grate the rind of 1 orange and the lemon and squeeze the juice from all the fruits. When the sugar has melted, add the grated rind and juice to the pan, together with any pulp from the fruit which is left in the squeezer. Increase the heat a little and stir the mixture until it comes to the boil. Add the brandy, if used, and cook for a further 1 minute.

If using for pancakes, have about 15 pancakes ready-made, folded in quarters. Put the folded pancakes into the sauce, one at a time, and turn them over to warm through. When all the pancakes have been heated, carefully lift them on to a serving plate and spoon over any excess sauce.

If using for pasta or over ice cream, thicken the sauce a little by adding 2 x 15 ml spoon (2 tablespoons) cornflour, mixed with 15 ml spoon (1 tablespoon) water. Cook for a further 5 minutes. Add 25 g (1 oz) flaked almonds if you like.

Cranberry and Orange Sauce

It always seems a shame that fresh cranberries are generally only available around Christmas time, but since this easy-to-make sauce freezes well, you can tuck away a good supply and enjoy it long beyond the festive season.

225 g	fresh cranberries	8 oz
1	large orange, quartered	1
2 x 15 ml spoon	caster sugar	2 tablespoons
a pinch	cinnamon (optional)	a pinch

Either coarsely grate the cranberries and orange (including the peel) or process both in a food processor. Mix in the sugar and cinnamon, if used. Leave to 'mellow' overnight in the refrigerator and use with turkey, chicken or ham.

Note: If you have a lot left over, make it into a jelly by stirring into a partially-set orange or lemon jelly. Serve with cold poultry or as a dessert, with cream.

Kumquat Purée

I usually prefer to keep kumquats whole, because they are so pretty, but here they are cut up to be puréed. This purée can be used in both savoury and sweet dishes, hot or cold.

175 g	sugar	6 oz
450 ml	water	¾ pint
350 g	kumquats, quartered, with the pips removed	12 oz

Dissolve the sugar in the water. Add the kumquats and cook, covered, until soft. Purée in a blender or food processor, and use as required (see below). This keeps well for a week or so in the refrigerator, well covered, or you can freeze it.

For savoury use, add 5 ml spoon (1 teaspoon) soya sauce to each 15 ml spoon (1 tablespoon) of the purée. Spread over grilled lamb or pork chops and brown under the grill, or use for barbecued meat. Use also as an accompaniment to roast pork, lamb or poultry.

For sweet use, spoon it, hot or cold, over ice cream, sorbet or plain cake; or use it as a topping for fruit salads and ice cream sundaes.

Jaffa French Dressing

6 x 15 ml spoon	oil (olive, corn or sunflower)	6 tablespoons
2 x 15 ml spoon	lemon or lime juice	2 tablespoons
5 ml spoon	mustard	1 teaspoon
a pinch	sugar	a pinch
	crushed garlic, to taste	
	salt and pepper	

Mix everything together well in a jar. Use as salad dressing.

Salads and Vegetables

'Meat and two veg.' is almost a music hall joke, but it is no laughing matter when vegetables are dull and soggy and salads are limp. This won't happen if you try some of the following quick tips for livening up the accompaniment to your meat.

Add a little grated orange, lemon or lime rind to any vegetable, or mix these into butter to make a flavoured topping. Form this grated rind and butter mixture into a roll and refrigerate or freeze, cutting into slices as required.

Make a Jaffa French Dressing (page 53) with extra garlic, and serve it over hot vegetables – carrots, cabbage, peas, courgettes – anything goes.

Add a squeeze of orange or lemon juice to the pan juices of sautéed vegetables, such as courgettes or mushrooms.

Serve vegetable purées in hollowed-out citrus shells – lemons or limes look nice, but oranges hold more.

A colourful and quickly-made salad of oranges and tomato slices, smothered in fresh basil, will win praises from everyone.

Instructions for making the following salads are brief (so that I can fit extra recipes in!), but who needs to be told how to combine the ingredients together? Just remember to leave the dressing until you serve the salad.

Carrot and Orange Salad

450 g	carrots, grated finely	1 lb
2	oranges, segmented and chopped	2
50 g	raisins	2 oz
	french dressing	

Combine everything together well.

Spinach and Orange Salad

175 g	spinach leaves, shredded (with the stalks removed)	6 oz
2	large oranges, segmented	2
50 g	hazelnuts, chopped coarsely	2 oz
3 x 15 ml spoon	natural yogurt	3 tablespoons
	salt and pepper	

Combine all the ingredients in a large bowl and mix thoroughly before serving. For a change, make a french dressing with hazelnut oil and use this instead of the yogurt.

Carrot Purée with Lime

Vegetable purées are always popular – maybe it's nostalgia for babyhood – but they are useful as well, since they can be made in advance and reheated.

450 g	carrots, sliced	1 lb
3 x 15 ml spoon	milk, heated	3 tablespoons
15 g	butter	½ oz
1	lime, juice of	1
	salt and pepper	

Cook the carrots until they are very soft. Drain them and put in a food processor or blender with the heated milk and butter. Process until smooth. Add the lime juice, salt and pepper and process again.

Most vegetables lend themselves to this preparation, and you can add either lemon or lime juice to highlight the flavours – try courgettes, brussels sprouts, cabbage, peas or celeriac.

Caraway Cabbage and Lemon

700 g	cabbage, shredded finely	1½ lb
40 g	butter	1½ oz
2	lemons, juice of	2
2 x 5 ml spoon	caraway seeds	2 teaspoons
	salt and pepper	

Put the cabbage in a heavy pan with all the remaining ingredients. Cook, covered, on a very low heat, stirring from time to time until the cabbage is just beginning to soften, but is still 'al dente'.

Any sort of cabbage is good with this – green, savoy, or white – or try using sliced brussels sprouts.

Green Beans in Orange Sauce

350 g	fresh green beans (runner, stick or french), with the strings removed	12 oz
15 ml spoon	oil	1 tablespoon
5 ml spoon	finely chopped fresh ginger root	1 teaspoon
200 ml	chicken stock	7 fl oz
2	large oranges, juice of	2
2 x 5 ml spoon	cornflour	2 teaspoons

Snap the beans into pieces about 2 cm (¾ inch) thick – leave french beans whole if they are thin. Heat the oil in a large frying pan or a wok. Add the chopped ginger and beans, and toss so that they are just coated with the oil. Add the chicken stock and cook until the liquid is nearly evaporated, by which time the beans should be 'al dente'. Mix the orange juice and cornflour together and add to the pan. Stir and cook for a further 2 minutes.

Coleslaw with Easy Peelers

450 g	white cabbage, shredded coarsely	1 lb
1	large carrot, grated	1
2	mineolas or topaz, segmented	2
3 x 15 ml spoon	mayonnaise	3 tablespoons
15 ml spoon	soured cream or yogurt	1 tablespoon
	salt and pepper	

Put the cabbage, carrot and segmented fruit in a large bowl. Mix together the mayonnaise and the soured cream or yogurt, add salt and pepper and pour into the bowl. Mix well.

Use orange segments if preferred.

Avocado and Grapefruit Salad

2	avocados, sliced	2
1	large grapefruit, segmented	1
	french dressing	

Combine everything together well. For a change, mix grapefruit and orange segments with the avocado. Or serve as a first course, with the avocado slices alternating with the fruit slices, on a bed of crisp salad.

Red Cabbage and Grapefruit

450 g	red cabbage, shredded finely	1 lb
2	small grapefruit, segmented	2
5 ml spoon	caraway seeds	1 teaspoon
	french dressing	

Combine all the ingredients together in a large bowl and mix well. Use 1 large pink grapefruit for a change, if preferred.

Spiced Parsnips with Orange

450 g	parsnips, cut into large dice	1 lb
1½ x 15 ml spoon	oil	1½ tablespoons
2.5 ml spoon	ground cumin	½ teaspoon
2.5 ml spoon	ground allspice	½ teaspoon
1	large orange, juice of	1
	salt	

Cook the parsnips in boiling water until they are just beginning to soften – don't overcook them. Drain well. Heat the oil in a large frying pan. Add the parsnips, the spices and salt and mix together carefully. Cook for 2 minutes, stirring gently. Add the orange juice and serve immediately.

Marrow with Dill and Lime

Marrow is not everyone's favourite vegetable, but I guarantee you'll convert the dubious with this Jaffa way – in fact, most people don't even realise it is marrow!

1	medium-size marrow	1
15 ml spoon	oil	1 tablespoon
5 ml spoon	dried dill weed	1 teaspoon
1	lime, juice of	1
	salt and pepper	

Peel the marrow and cut into 1 cm (½-inch) slices, discarding the seeds. Heat the oil in a large frying pan or a wok and cook the marrow until it begins to soften and is taking on a little colour. Sprinkle on the dill and lime juice and season to taste. Stir well and serve immediately. (This could, of course, be cooked with courgettes.)

Minted Jaffa Red Blush and Chinese Leaves

450 g	chinese leaves, shredded coarsely	1 lb
2	Red Blush or Sunrise grapefruit, segmented and halved	2
3 x 15 ml spoon	chopped fresh mint french dressing	3 tablespoons

Combine everything together well.

Orange, Onion and Olive Salad

4	large oranges, sliced thinly	4
225 g	spanish or red-skinned onions, sliced thinly	8 oz
6 x 15 ml spoon	olive oil	6 tablespoons
3 x 15 ml spoon	lemon juice	3 tablespoons
2 x 15 ml spoon	chopped parsley	2 tablespoons
50 g	black olives salt and pepper	2 oz

Put the sliced orange and sliced onion in a bowl. Combine the oil, lemon juice, parsley, salt and pepper together well and pour over the orange and onion. Remove the stones from the olives, halve and decorate the salad with them.

Jaffa Fennel Salad

450 g	fennel, with plenty of green fern, sliced into thin sticks	1 lb
2	mineolas or topaz, sliced thickly and halved french dressing	2

Combine everything together, using all the green fern from the fennel for extra colour. You can also make this with orange segments, for a change.

Minted Jaffa Red Blush and Chinese Leaves; Orange, Onion and Olive Salad; Jaffa Fennel Salad

Desserts

It will not escape the eagle-eyed that many of these recipes for desserts are variations on a theme of egg, sugar and citrus fruit, with or without cream. What is fascinating, to me and I hope to you, is how different the same basic ingredients can taste when combined and prepared in different ways.

For the more abstemious (or sensible?), Jaffa fruit unadorned makes the perfect no-fat dessert, and many recipes are easily in the low fat category. For instance, use the shells of grapefruit or oranges to hold citrus fruit salad, and top them with meringue, baked until golden brown.

Here are a few more rapid ways to brighten the end of the meal:

Add a squeeze of lime or lemon to melon balls, and serve well chilled. Add a sliver of lemon or orange rind to a sugar syrup for fruit salad.

The Jaffa omelette, with fruit or marmalade (page 15), makes a super dessert.

Grill oranges (prepared as for grilled grapefruit on page 14), sprinkled with spices such as ginger, cinnamon or mixed spices and brown sugar.

Add grated citrus rind to a butter biscuit mixture for citrus biscuits.

Add a sliver of lemon rind to apples when making apple sauce.

Syllabub

Although a syllabub was originally made with wine, non-alcoholic syllabubs are perhaps even nicer, especially with the tang of citrus.

300 ml	double cream	½ pint
50 g	caster sugar	2 oz
175 ml	citrus fruit juice	6 fl oz
	grated rind	

Combine the cream, sugar and juice in a large bowl and whip together until light and thick. Spoon into glasses and chill for a few hours, until required. Decorate with some grated rind or some finely chopped pistachios.

Use any single fruit, or a combination of different fruits: grapefruit, orange and lemon; lemon and lime; mineola and lemon; topaz and grapefruit; orange and lemon . . . ad infinitum!

Gin and Lime Posset

A posset is a lighter version of a syllabub.

225 ml	double cream	8 fl oz
110 ml	lime juice	4 fl oz
	grated lime rind	
3 x 15 ml spoon	caster sugar	3 tablespoons
2 x 15 ml spoon	gin	2 tablespoons
2	egg whites	2
6	thin slices of lime, to garnish	6

Combine the cream, lime juice, grated rind, caster sugar and gin in a large bowl and whip until thick. In a separate bowl, beat the egg whites until stiff. Take a large spoonful of the whites and fold into the cream mixture to lighten it. Fold in the rest of the whites. Mix very gently to incorporate the two mixtures. Spoon into six glasses and refrigerate until required – up to 3 hours. Decorate each glass with a slice of lime.

You can omit the gin if you prefer, or make a lemon posset in the same way, adding brandy instead of the gin if you like.

Lemon Roulade

Chocolate roulades are always gobbled up at parties but I think this lemon version makes a delightful change. It was created by Ann Norris for her cookery school near Bath.

100 g	curd cheese	4 oz
4	eggs, separated	4
150 g	caster sugar	5 oz
2	large lemons	2
225 g	raspberries, defrosted if frozen	8 oz
	icing sugar	
300 ml	whipping cream, whipped	½ pint

Beat the curd cheese, egg yolks and caster sugar together until pale – at least 5 minutes in an electric beater. Add the grated zest of both the lemons and the juice of just one half. Mix thoroughly.

Stiffly beat the egg whites and fold a spoonful into the yolk mixture to lighten it before adding the rest and mixing through gently.

Line a swiss roll tin, measuring 38 x 25 cm (15 x 10 inches), with lightly oiled greaseproof paper. Turn the mixture into the tin, smoothing into the edges. Bake at 170°C/325°F/Gas Mark 3 for 25–30 minutes, until it is lightly browned. Place a damp cloth on top of the sponge and leave it to cool.

Make the raspberry purée: sieve the raspberries and add icing sugar to taste. Sprinkle some icing sugar on to a clean tea-towel and turn the sponge on to it. Carefully peel away the greaseproof paper, easing it off gently as the sponge is very fragile. Spread very carefully with the whipped cream and, using the tea-towel to help you, lift the shorter edge of the sponge up until it rolls over. Continue until the roll is completed. Dredge the roll with icing sugar.

To serve: put a thin layer of the raspberry purée on to each plate. Cut a slice of the roulade and carefully place it in the centre of the plate.

Sorbets

Sorbets are very easy to make by hand, and easier still if you have an ice cream machine. Beating the frozen mixture twice makes it smoother, but you can omit the second beating if you wish. Purists will tell you that a real sorbet doesn't contain egg whites, but I have seen many recipes that do and just as many that don't, so you can call it whatever you like. All sorbets serve 4.

Citrus fruit is perhaps the most commonly used ingredient for sorbets, but many recipes for other flavoured sorbets contain lemon juice, since it helps to heighten flavours. These recipes are purely citrus sorbets. The same method applies whichever fruits you choose.

Lemon Sorbet

600 ml	water	1 pint
225 g	sugar	8 oz
2	lemons, grated rind of	2
225 ml	lemon juice	8 fl oz
2	egg whites	2

Make a syrup by boiling the water with the sugar for 5 minutes. Cool and then mix with the grated rind and juice. Pour into a shallow container and freeze until it is firm around the edges (the time depends on your freezer). Remove from the freezer and mix in a blender or food processor, or by hand. Return the mixture to the freezer and freeze again until firm.

Repeat the mixing in the blender as above but this time stiffly beat the egg whites and add to the mixture. Return to the freezer and leave until firm. If it becomes too hard, leave the sorbet at room temperature for 15 minutes before serving.

Empty lemon or lime shells make pretty containers for sorbet — choose large fruit, and fill with the sorbet after the egg white has been added.

Lime Sorbet

Substitute lime juice and rind for the lemon juice and make as for Lemon Sorbet.

Mineola Sorbet

Make a syrup of 50 g (2 oz) sugar and 150 ml (¼ pint) water. Grate some rind from 2 mineolas and add to the cooled syrup, together with 300 ml (½ pint) mineola juice and the juice of 1 lemon. Freeze and add 1 beaten egg white as for Lemon Sorbet.

Mixed Citrus Sorbet

Make a syrup of 50g (2 oz) sugar with 150 ml (¼ pint) water. Squeeze the juice from 1 grapefruit (preferably Red Blush or Sunrise) and 2 lemons and then add orange juice to make up to 450 ml (¾ pint). Add some grated rind. Freeze and add 1 beaten egg white as for Lemon Sorbet.

Citrus Strudel

Real strudel involves a lot of hard work — not, I'm afraid, very appealing to those short of time. Here's a mock strudel that uses ready-bought pastry. It is the sort of dessert you could whistle up with store cupboard ingredients.

200 g	puff pastry, defrosted if frozen	7 oz
40 g	cornflakes, crushed lightly	1½ oz
2	large grapefruit, segmented	2
40 g	walnuts or pecans, chopped	1½ oz
2 x 15 ml spoon	light muscovado sugar	2 tablespoons
1½ x 15 ml spoon	butter, cut into dice	1½ tablespoons
1	beaten egg, for glazing	1

Roll the pastry out as thinly as you can. Sprinkle the crushed cornflakes over the top. Pat the grapefruit segments dry with kitchen paper towelling and lay them on the cornflakes. Scatter the nuts and sugar on top and then the pieces of butter. Roll up carefully and lift the roll on to a moistened baking sheet. Brush with the beaten egg. Bake at 190°C/375°F/Gas Mark 5 for about 25 minutes, until golden brown.

Slide off the baking sheet and leave to cool for just a few minutes before serving, perhaps with whipped cream or ice cream.

You could substitute some orange for one of the grapefruit if you like.

Sunrise Special

The London Jaffa office volunteered this wonderful way with the wonderful Sunrise grapefruit. It is just as good with Red Blush — and not at all bad with old-fashioned yellow grapefruit!

2	Sunrise grapefruit, segmented	2
2 x 15 ml spoon	orange liqueur	2 tablespoons
	(Grand Marnier or similar)	
	dark brown muscovado sugar	

Place the grapefruit segments in a shallow heatproof dish. Sprinkle on the liqueur and just enough sugar to cover lightly. Preheat the grill to a high heat and then grill the grapefruit until the sugar begins to caramelise and turn black. Remove from the grill and cool, then refrigerate, overnight if possible.

I serve this with whipped cream, which scandalised the person who gave me the recipe — but it is deliciously sinful.

Flambéed Pomelo

Bring some drama into your life with a (carefully controlled) flambé, either at your table, or (just as acceptable) over the kitchen stove.

1	pomelo, segmented	1
25 g	butter	1 oz
2 x 15 ml spoon	demerara sugar	2 tablespoons
3 x 15 ml spoon	white rum or orange liqueur	3 tablespoons

Try to keep the pomelo segments as large as possible, as they disintegrate when heated. In a large frying pan melt the butter, but don't let it brown. Add the pomelo segments and sugar and warm through gently for 2 minutes. Put the rum or liqueur into a soup ladle and warm it. Ignite and pour over the pomelo, shaking the pan. Take to the table while still flaming and serve immediately.

St Clement's Soufflé

Any mixture of oranges and lemons inevitably becomes dubbed 'St Clement's', after the nursery rhyme. Soufflés are impressive, and rightly so, for they do look and taste extra special. But those in the know are keeping a well guarded secret – that they are really very easy to make.

4	egg yolks	4
175 g	caster sugar	6 oz
25 g	plain flour	1 oz
450 ml	milk, scalded	¾ pint
50 ml	orange juice	2 fl oz
50 ml	lemon juice	2 fl oz
	grated orange and lemon rind	
6	egg whites	6
15 ml spoon	icing sugar	1 tablespoon

Beat the egg yolks with the caster sugar. Stir in the flour. Scald the milk and add to the egg mixture, beating continually. Cook on a low heat, whisking all the time until the mixture begins to thicken. Continue cooking for 3 minutes, stirring continually. Cool the mixture and add the juices and rinds.

Whisk the whites until stiff. Put a spoonful of the whites into the milk mixture to lighten it a little, then carefully fold in the remaining whites. Turn the mixture into a greased 2-litre (3½-pint) soufflé dish. Bake at 190°C/375°F/Gas Mark 5 for 30 minutes. Sprinkle lightly with the icing sugar and serve IMMEDIATELY. Soufflés, like time, wait for no man.

Make this with just orange or just lemon, or use another citrus fruit – lime or mineola perhaps.

Lemon Meringue Pie

The filling for a real, home-made lemon meringue pie (as opposed to one from a packet) is rather like a lemon curd, and any citrus curd could be substituted for the lemon in this pie.

3	eggs, beaten	3
200 g	caster sugar	7 oz
100 g	butter, diced	4 oz
110 ml	lemon juice	4 fl oz
	grated lemon rind	
1	ready-baked pastry case (18 cm/7-inch)	1
2	egg whites	2
a pinch	cream of tartar	a pinch
4 x 15 ml spoon	caster sugar	4 tablespoons

In the top of a double boiler, combine the beaten eggs, the 200 g (7 oz) caster sugar, butter, lemon juice and grated rind. (If you do not have a double boiler, set a bowl over a saucepan half full of water.) Cook over simmering water, stirring continually until a thick custard has formed. Remove from the heat and cool a little.

Turn the custard into the baked pastry case. Beat the egg whites with the cream of tartar until very stiff. Slowly add the caster sugar to make a stiff meringue. Cover the pie with the meringue, taking care to seal the edges of the pie with it. Bake in the oven at 170°C/325°F/Gas Mark 3 for 15 minutes, until the top is lightly browned. Cool and then refrigerate until required.

If preferred, you can make a biscuit crumb base with 75 g (3 oz) crushed digestive biscuits mixed with 25 g (1 oz) melted butter, pressed into the bottom of a small, spring-form tin. To make a lime pie, proceed as above, substituting lime juice for lemon. When the filling is cold, cover with 75 ml (3 fl oz) whipped double cream, instead of the meringue.

Jaffa Trifle

There's a distinctly Mediterranean taste to this essentially English dish which I hope may please even the purist.

3–4	mineolas or topaz	3–4
1½	packets of chocolate-topped orange cakes	1½
4	egg yolks	4
3 x 15 ml spoon	caster sugar	3 tablespoons
2 x 15 ml spoon	cornflour	2 tablespoons
600 ml	milk	1 pint
150 ml	double cream, whipped	¼ pint

Squeeze the juice from 2–3 of the mineolas or topaz to make 200 ml (7 fl oz), and pour into a shallow dish. Dip the cake side of each of the orange cakes into the juice. Place them, chocolate side up, in a shallow glass bowl, in one layer if possible or cut to fit the bottom. Pour any excess juice over the cakes.

Make the custard: mix the egg yolks, sugar, cornflour and some grated rind from the mineola or topaz with a little milk. Heat the remaining milk and pour it on to the egg mixture, stirring briskly. Return the mixture to the pan and cook over a low heat until thickened and just beginning to boil, stirring constantly. Pour over the orange cakes immediately. Leave to cool, then cover with the whipped cream and decorate with segments of the remaining mineola or topaz.

Candied Kumquats

For a special occasion these make a very luxurious dessert on their own, but you can economise and make half the recipe to serve with ice cream, or a mousse.

Candied Kumquats; Jaffa Trifle

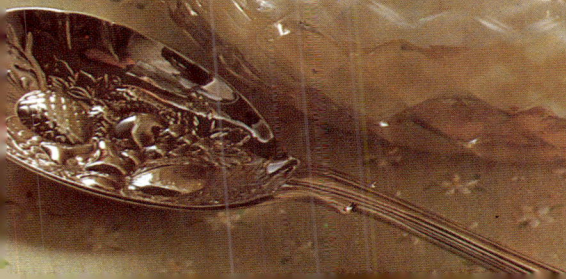

450 g	kumquats	1 lb
225 g	sugar	8 oz
300 ml	water	½ pint
1	stick of cinnamon	1

Put the kumquats in a pan and cover them with water. Bring to the boil and simmer, covered, for 15 minutes. Drain and prick the kumquats with a toothpick. Dissolve the sugar in the measured water in a pan. Add the cinnamon stick and kumquats. Bring to the boil, putting a plate on the kumquats to keep them under the liquid. Cover the pan and simmer for 20 minutes. Cool and then refrigerate until required. Serve very cold, with whipped cream if desired.

These candied kumquats can be preserved in brandy. Cook as above, drain and reserve the liquid and put the kumquats in a sterilised jar. Pour in brandy, to fill three-quarters of the jar. Top up with the reserved liquid. Keep in a cool, dark place for at least two weeks. Eat and enjoy (one at a time is usually enough). Use the brandy for flavouring cream or sauces, when all the kumquats have been eaten.

Sweet Jaffa Salads

With a few pieces of citrus fruit in the house you need never be without a delicious and nutritious dessert, for family meals or elegant dinners. All salads serve 4.

Orange Date and Almond Salad

3	oranges, segmented, plus any juice from the cutting	3
175 g	fresh dates, quartered and stoned	6 oz
25 g	flaked almonds	1 oz
15 ml spoon	orange flower water	1 tablespoon

Combine everything together and serve, well chilled.

Spicy Orange Salad

6	oranges, peeled and sliced thinly	6
200 ml	red wine	7 fl oz
6 x 15 ml spoon	sugar	6 tablespoons
1	stick of cinnamon	1
4	cloves	4

Put the sliced oranges into a heatproof dish. Combine all the remaining ingredients with a sliver of orange rind, put in a saucepan and heat just to the boil, then simmer for 5 minutes. Pour over the oranges and serve either hot or cold.

Orange Slices
Sprinkle slices of orange with sugar and ground cinnamon and a little orange flower water – you could make orange baskets and fill them with this mixture.

Caramel Oranges
This is an old favourite: put together slices of orange covered with caramelised rind (page 8). Serve well chilled, with some liqueur added to the syrup – whisky liqueur makes an interesting change from orange liqueur.

Orange Segments
Segment large oranges and arrange them attractively on a serving dish. Serve well chilled, completely unadorned – they make a fresh, clean end to a rich meal.

Oranges and Strawberries
Combine segmented oranges and sliced strawberries, or simply sprinkle orange juice over fresh strawberries.

Mixed Citrus Salads
Combine any citrus fruits you have available, adding some sugar syrup which has been boiled with a sliver of lemon or orange rind. Add other tropical fruits, for a change – kiwifruit, mango, sharon fruit, pineapple – either one to one, or a mixture of whatever is available.

Orange Soured Cream Cake

4	eggs	4
100 g	caster sugar	4 oz
50 g	plain flour	2 oz
50 g	cornflour	2 oz
5 ml spoon	baking powder	1 teaspoon
225 ml	orange juice, strained	8 fl oz
300 ml	soured cream	½ pint
4 x 15 ml spoon	icing sugar	4 tablespoons
3 x 15 ml spoon	orange juice and pulp	3 tablespoons
	grated orange rind, blanched (page 8)	

First, make the cake. Beat the eggs and the caster sugar together until very light and frothy (about 5 minutes by machine). Sieve the flour, cornflour and baking powder on to the egg mixture and very gently fold in, mixing through lightly to incorporate the dry ingredients. Turn into a lightly greased 20 cm (8-inch) tin (spring-form if possible), and bake at 170°C/325°F/Gas Mark 3 for 45 minutes.

Cool the cake and then cut in half. Pour half of the strained orange juice over each half of the cake. Mix the soured cream, icing sugar and the orange juice with pulp together well. Spread half on the bottom layer of the cake. Cover with the second half of the cake and then spread the rest of the soured cream mixture on top. Sprinkle or arrange the blanched orange rind to decorate. Freeze for 3–4 hours. Remove from the freezer 10 minutes before eating.

If you want to freeze this for longer, allow more time out of the freezer before serving – it should be very cold but not frozen solid.

Orange Soured Cream Cake; Orange Cream

Orange Cream

This could be called a 'four in one' recipe because I have given four super versions of the one basic idea — and they are all delicious!

3	egg yolks	3
175 g	caster sugar	6 oz
175 ml	orange juice	6 fl oz
1	lemon, juice and grated rind of	1
2 x 5 ml spoon	gelatine	2 teaspoons
2 x 15 ml spoon	water	2 tablespoons
300 ml	double cream, whipped	½ pint
	poached orange slices or caramelised rind, to decorate (page 8)	

Mix the egg yolks, sugar, orange juice, lemon juice and grated rind together in a saucepan and cook over a low heat for about 8 minutes, stirring constantly. Do not boil. The sauce should thicken slightly. While this is cooking, soak the gelatine in the water. Stir the soaked gelatine into the hot mixture until it dissolves.

Sieve the mixture into a bowl, set in a larger bowl of crushed ice if possible (I use frozen freezer packs in a bowl of water, as they don't melt). Stir the mixture until it begins to set. (You can leave the mixture in the fridge until this point, but make sure that you catch it before it has set.)

Fold the whipped cream into the setting mixture, mixing through well. Pour into a moistened 1-litre (1¾-pint) mould and refrigerate until set, preferably overnight. Turn out and decorate with the poached orange slices or caramelised rind. This freezes well.

You may like to colour the mixture with orange food colouring, to make it a darker orange.

Variation 1 Make a Lemon Cream by using 150 ml (¼ pint) lemon juice and grated lemon rind instead of the orange. Decorate with poached lemon slices or twists of lemon.

Variation 2   Make an Orange Cream or Lemon Cream as above, but fold in 3 stiffly beaten egg whites after the whipped cream. Turn the mixture into a bowl and leave to set, decorating as above.

Variation 3   For a party, make a very attractive double-flavoured cream by setting the Orange Cream in a large mould and then setting the Lemon Cream on top. Unmould and decorate with alternate slices of orange and lemon (in this case, colour the Orange Cream with food colouring, to make a contrast).

Jaffa Valentine

I originally devised this cream to use as the filling for a heart-shaped meringue case, for St Valentine's Day, but found it just as tasty as a filling for pastry or to top a trifle.

2	large grapefruit	2
5 x 5 ml spoon	cornflour	5 teaspoons
3	egg yolks	3
75 g	caster sugar	3 oz
150 ml	double cream	¼ pint

Grate the rind of one of the grapefruit and squeeze the juice. Mix the grated rind and juice with the cornflour. Put the egg yolks in a small saucepan and add the cornflour mixture and the sugar. Mix everything together well with a whisk and place over a low heat. Continue stirring while the mixture begins to thicken, scraping the bottom of the pan. Keep the heat very low. Cook until the mixture is very thick, about 4 minutes. Turn the mixture into a bowl and leave to cool.

Peel the second grapefruit and segment it, cutting each piece in two. Fold the cut fruit into the cooled mixture. Whip the cream and fold this into the grapefruit mixture. Spoon into a meringue shell or baked pastry case, or use as you wish.

If you do want to make a heart-shaped meringue, colour this filling a delicate pink with a few drops of red food colouring.

Jaffa Gratin

Good recipes travel well. I first had this in a London restaurant, *Mijanou*, but later rediscovered it at Roger Vergé's *Moulin de Mougins* in the South of France.

1	grapefruit, segmented	1
1	orange, segmented with the rind cut into matchsticks and blanched (page 8)	1
1	topaz, segmented	1
1	mineola	1
2	egg yolks	2
5 x 15 ml spoon	caster sugar	5 tablespoons
3 x 15 ml spoon	orange juice	3 tablespoons

Arrange the segments of the different fruits on four gratin dishes (or any heatproof shallow dish). Sprinkle half of the sugar over the fruit.

In a bowl, combine the egg yolks, the rest of the sugar and the orange juice. Mix well and place the bowl over a pan of boiling water on a medium heat. Keep whisking the contents of the bowl until the mixture becomes light and frothy (you are in effect making a *zabaglione* type sauce). Remove the bowl from the heat and add the blanched orange rind.

Spoon the egg mixture over the fruit segments and place under a preheated grill for a few seconds to colour lightly. Serve immediately.

You can, if you prefer, use all the same citrus fruit, or whatever mixture you like. The egg mixture has to be prepared just before serving as it deflates very quickly.

Sussex Pond Pudding

One of the glories of British cooking is the steamed pudding, and few are more delicious than this curiously named one. You can see where the pond comes into it, but I'm not too sure about Sussex.

225 g	self-raising flour	8 oz
a pinch	salt	a pinch
100 g	shredded suet	4 oz
approx. 175 ml	mixture of milk and water	approx. 6 fl oz
150 g	butter, diced	5 oz
150 g	demerara sugar	5 oz
1	large lemon, thin-skinned if possible	1

First make the crust: mix the flour, salt and suet together and add just enough of the milk and water mixture to make a soft dough. Knead the dough on a lightly-floured board and then roll it out to a thickness of about 5 mm (¼ inch). Cut off a quarter of the dough and use the rest to line a greased 900 ml (1½-pint) pudding basin.

Put half of the diced butter in the bottom of the lined basin and add half of the sugar. Prick the lemon all over with a skewer and place it on the butter and sugar. Cover with the remaining butter and sugar and then put on the lid of reserved dough, moistening the edges and pressing to seal the edges. Cover with a double layer of greased paper, leaving a pleat in the paper for the pudding to rise.

Place the pudding basin on a trivet in a pan half filled with boiling water. Cover the pan and boil for about 4 hours, topping up the boiling water in the pan when necessary. Turn the pudding out on to a deep serving dish.

Lemon Mousse

A light, relatively low calorie dessert, this always wins praise. Try the different versions given below, to ring the changes.

3	eggs, separated	3
3 x 15 ml spoon	caster sugar	3 tablespoons
2 x 5 ml spoon	gelatine	2 teaspoons
2 x 15 ml spoon	boiling water	2 tablespoons
110 ml	lemon juice	4 fl oz
	grated lemon rind	
4	thin twists of lemon, to decorate	4

Beat the egg yolks with the sugar until light and creamy. Dissolve the gelatine in the boiling water and strain on to the yolks, beating all the time. Add the lemon juice and grated rind and mix well.

Beat the egg whites until they are very stiff. Carefully fold a large spoonful of the whites into the yolks to lighten the mixture, and then fold in the remaining whites. Spoon into a large bowl or four individual glasses or bowls. Refrigerate until required. Decorate with twists of lemon.

Grapefruit Mousse: use a large grapefruit to make 110 ml (4 fl oz) juice and include the pulp left in the squeezer, without the pips.

Mineola or Topaz Mousse: squeeze enough mineolas or topaz to give you 225 ml (8 fl oz) juice. Increase the gelatine to 15 ml spoon (1 tablespoon). As the mousse begins to set, fold in some chopped segments of the fruit.

For a richer version of all these mousses, increase the gelatine by a further 5 ml spoon (1 teaspoon), and fold in 300 ml (½ pint) whipping cream, whipped, before adding the egg whites.

Frozen Jaffa Cream

It is always useful to have a delicious dessert in the freezer for an emergency, and nothing could be nicer than this lovely creamy soufflé, which actually doesn't have any cream in it!

75 ml	lemon juice	3 fl oz
75 ml	orange juice	3 fl oz
	grated orange and lemon rind	
50 g	granulated sugar	2 oz
4	egg yolks	4
3	egg whites	3
50 g	caster sugar	2 oz

Combine the lemon juice, orange juice and grated rinds in a heavy saucepan with the granulated sugar and egg yolks. Beat well and place the pan on a low heat, stirring continually until the mixture becomes thick and glutinous. Don't let it overheat, as the yolks will scramble. Remove the pan from the heat and plunge it into a basin of cold water to cool the mixture quickly and prevent it cooking further.

Whisk the egg whites until they are very stiff. Fold in the caster sugar and mix through. Take a spoonful of the whites and fold into the yolk mixture to lighten it. Add the rest of the beaten whites and mix in gently but thoroughly. Spoon the mixture into a serving dish (a small soufflé dish will do), cover it with foil and freeze for a minimum of 6 hours. It will keep for a month in the freezer. Serve straight from the freezer.

You can decorate this, just before serving, with caramelised rind (page 8).

Orange Chocolate Frosting

Jazz up your favourite chocolate cake by covering it with this orange chocolate frosting.

225 g	icing sugar	8 oz
100 g	butter	4 oz
50 ml	orange juice	2 fl oz
	grated orange rind, to taste	
2 x 15 ml spoon	cocoa	2 tablespoons
2 x 15 ml spoon	boiling water	2 tablespoons

In a food processor or large bowl, mix together the icing sugar and butter until smooth. Add the orange juice and rind and mix in. Mix the cocoa and boiling water together to a smooth paste and add to the bowl. Mix well. Spread in the middle and on top of chocolate cake.

Lemon Icing

A quick way to liven up a plain cake is to cover it with a tangy lemon icing. Use it also for rich fruit cake, or lemon or chocolate cake. Make an orange icing in the same way.

50 ml	lemon juice	2 fl oz
	grated lemon rind, to taste	
200–225 g	icing sugar, sieved	7–8 oz

In a large bowl, mix the juice and rind with the sugar (added a spoonful at a time), mixing with a fork until smooth – add just enough sugar to make a spreadable consistency. Pour on to the cake and smooth over with a metal spatula that has been dipped into hot water.

Preserves and Drinks

Breakfast wouldn't be breakfast without marmalade, and a gin and tonic wouldn't be the drink it is without a slice of lemon, so this is a most essential part of the book!

The preserves here range from the essential breakfast confection to the more exotic spiced kumquats. I was happily surprised to discover that you don't need masses of any fruit to make some lovely pickles and preserves – just a few oranges can make a sparkling jar of spiced fruit – and all the peel you might once have thrown away you will now certainly use to make candied peel. Preserves also make wonderful presents, thoughtful and delicious.

No self-respecting cocktail shaker would be without his/her oranges, lemons and limes, but for the non-alcoholic, help is at hand – try hot milk with brown sugar and orange juice, or hot chocolate with grated orange peel and a slice of orange. That should cure something!

Marmalade
Citrus fruit is, of course, synonymous with marmalade and I have thoroughly enjoyed making every possible variety of this most indispensable breakfast confection. If, like me, you have always limited your marmalade making to oranges, treat yourself to all these possible variations. You don't need to make vast quantities – just a few pieces of fruit can yield 3 or 4 jars of marmalade. The same method applies to any fruit you choose.

Pomelo Marmalade
Yields about 3.5 kg/7½ lb.

900 g	pomelo	2 lb
2.8 litres	water	5 pints
2.25 kg	sugar	5 lb
2	lemons, juice of	2

You may find that 1 pomelo weighs more than you need for this recipe, so cut off any extra and use as you wish. Discard any pips.

Cut the pomelo into wedges and slice thinly. Put these slices in a large pan (a preserving pan if possible) together with the measured water. Leave to soak overnight. The next day, simmer the contents of the pan, covered, until the peel is soft. The time for this obviously depends on how thinly you have cut the fruit, but may take up to 1½ hours, so keep your eye on it.

Warm the sugar in the oven if possible before adding to the fruit. Then add the lemon juice and stir round until the sugar is dissolved. Bring to the boil and boil rapidly without stirring, until setting point is reached. This may take quite a long time – anything from about 20 minutes, but keep testing, so as not to overcook it – it should set firmly on a plate when it is cold, forming a skin when pushed with your finger. Take the pan off the heat while waiting for each test to set. Let the marmalade cool a little before pouring into hot, clean jars. To sterilise jars, heat them in the oven while you are heating the sugar. Make sure that they are completely dry before filling.

Lemon Marmalade
Make as above, but with 450 g (1 lb) lemons, 1.5 litres (2½ pints) water and 1.2 kg (2½ lb) sugar. Yields about 2 kg/4 lb.

Lime Marmalade
Substitute limes for lemons as above.

Lemon and Lime Marmalade
Combine the two recipes above. Yields about 3.5 kg/7½ lb.

Grapefruit Marmalade
Substitute grapefruit for lemons as in Lemon Marmalade, and add the juice of 1 lemon.

Mineola Marmalade
Make as for Pomelo Marmalade, but with 450 g (1 lb) mineolas, the juice of 1 lemon, 900 ml (1½ pints) water and 700 g (1½ lb) sugar. Yields about 900 g/2 lb.

Orange and Lemon Marmalade

Make as for Pomelo Marmalade, but with 450 g (1 lb) oranges, 450 g (1 lb) lemons, 2 litres (3½ pints) water and 1.4 kg (3 lb) sugar. Yields about 2.5 kg/5 lb.

Fruit Curds

Fruit curds are delightfully delicate and pretty, too. My own favourite is lemon curd, but any citrus fruit can be used. Remember, though, that they don't have the kind of shelf life that other conserves have, so keep in the refrigerator and use within a few weeks for the best flavour. Small jars of curd make a welcome gift. This basic recipe will do for all the variations; just change the quantities as shown.

Lemon Curd

4	lemons, grated rind of	4
175 ml	lemon juice	6 fl oz
225 g	sugar	8 oz
100 g	unsalted butter	4 oz
2	eggs, beaten	2

Put the grated lemon rind, lemon juice, sugar and butter in the top of a double saucepan or in a basin set over hot water. Cook, stirring from time to time, until the sugar has dissolved and the butter melted.

Add the beaten eggs and continue cooking until the mixture thickens and coats the back of a wooden spoon. Fill cleaned and dried jars and seal when cool.

Use as a spread or as a filling for tarts. This makes lovely individual tartlets: put a teaspoon of curd in a baked pastry case, top with a swirl of meringue and bake for 5 minutes.

Lime Curd

Substitute limes for lemons in the same quantity.

Orange Curd

Use the grated rind of 2 oranges, 175 ml (6 fl oz) orange juice, 225 g (8 oz) sugar, 100 g (4 oz) unsalted butter and 2 eggs.

Orange and Lemon Curd

Use the grated rind of 1 lemon and 2 oranges, 110 ml (4 fl oz) orange juice, 50 ml (2 fl oz) lemon juice, 225 g (8 oz) sugar, 100 g (4 oz) unsalted butter and 2 eggs.

Spiced Oranges or Kumquats

Spiced oranges or kumquats make a tangy accompaniment to cold meats and poultry. The same method works for both fruits.

	either	
450 g	kumquats	1 lb
	or	
3	large oranges, sliced	3
275 g	sugar	10 oz
300 ml	wine vinegar	½ pint
1	stick of cinnamon	1
6	whole cloves	6
15 ml spoon	coriander seeds	1 tablespoon

Prick the kumquats with a toothpick and put them in a pan with water to cover, or put the orange slices in a pan with water to cover. Simmer until the kumquats begin to soften (but not collapse) or the orange skin begins to soften. Drain the fruit, reserving the liquid.

Dissolve the sugar in the vinegar. Add all the spices and bring to the boil. Add the drained fruit and put a plate over the fruit to keep it under the liquid. Simmer until the rind looks transparent – about 25 minutes.

Put the fruit in a sterilised jar. Pour on the syrup, to cover the fruit completely. Top up with the reserved liquid if necessary (it is essential that the fruit is completely covered). Cover the jar with a non-metal lid and leave in a cool, dark place for about a month.

Mineola Marmalade; Lemon Curd; Spiced Oranges; Candied Peel

Candied Peel

There is no gift more popular than a home-made one. I have found that children love making this candied peel, packing it into pretty boxes and giving it at Christmas and birthdays to grandmothers and aunts (and maybe even to mother!). Soft citrus (easy peelers) aren't any good for this, but pomelo peel is ideal.

225 g	citrus peel (mixed or just one variety)	8 oz
225 g	granulated sugar	8 oz
15 ml spoon	golden syrup	1 tablespoon
300 ml	water	½ pint
	granulated sugar, to roll the cooked peel in	

Use Shamouti rather than Navel oranges if possible. Pomelo peel is very thick, so you should remove the soft pith (which scrapes away quite easily after the peel has been boiled), otherwise it won't dry crisp and hard.

Try to have large pieces of peel if possible, without any fruit flesh on it but with the pith. Put the peel in a saucepan and cover with cold water. Bring to the boil, reduce the heat and simmer for 10 minutes. Drain off the water and repeat the boiling and simmering of the peel in fresh water two more times (three times in all). After the third cooking, drain the peel and leave it to cool for a few minutes. Cut into strips about 3 mm (⅛ inch) wide.

Put the measured sugar and golden syrup in a pan with the measured water. Stir while the sugar dissolves. Add the peel to the pan and bring the contents of the pan to the boil, stirring carefully. Reduce the heat and boil gently – not rapidly. Cook for about 30 minutes, during which time the liquid will be absorbed. Take care that the liquid doesn't boil away. Remove the peel from the pan and cool on a plate for 10 minutes.

Sprinkle some granulated sugar on to a board and roll the peel to coat it, a few pieces at a time. Leave the sugared peel on a plate to dry, uncovered, for about two days in a warm place. When it is quite dry and stiff, store in an airtight tin. It keeps for 2–3 weeks (unless eaten!).

Jaffa Chutney
Makes about 1 kg/2 lb

4	grapefruit, peeled and sliced	4
2	oranges, peeled and sliced	2
1	lemon, peeled and sliced	1
450 g	onions, sliced thinly	1 lb
4 x 5 ml spoon	salt	4 teaspoons
350 g	light muscovado sugar	12 oz
450 ml	vinegar	¾ pint
15 ml spoon	mustard seeds	1 tablespoon
5 ml spoon	ground ginger	1 teaspoon
5 ml spoon	ground cinnamon	1 teaspoon
2.5 ml spoon	chilli powder	½ teaspoon

Discard any pips from the fruit. Put all the fruit in a large bowl with the sliced onions and the salt. Cover and leave overnight.

Put the contents of the bowl in a large pan and add the remaining ingredients. Slowly bring to the boil, stirring constantly. Reduce the heat and simmer very gently, stirring from time to time, until the mixture is mushy and most of the liquid has evaporated. This should be done very slowly – it may take up to an hour or more.

Fill cold, sterilised jars and, when cool, cover with plastic lids (the vinegar will corrode metal tops).

Lemonade

4	lemons	4
50 g	caster sugar	2 oz
900 ml	boiling water	1½ pints

Remove the rind (without the pith) from 2 of the lemons and put in a large jug with the sugar. Pour over the boiling water and leave to cool, stirring from time to time. Add the juice of all the lemons and refrigerate until required. Strain before serving and add ice cubes and more sugar to taste, if necessary.

Make Limeade in the same way, substituting limes.

Real Planters' Punch

> 'One part sour,
> Two parts sweet.
> Three parts strong
> And four parts weak.'

(As told by a West Indian friend, in rhyme.)

Translated you need: 1 part lime, 2 parts sugar syrup, 3 parts rum and 4 parts soda and ice. Mix together, stir well – and enjoy.

Buck's Fizz
Makes 1 glass

This is the perfect party drink for early morning, midday or evening revelries – and for those who don't like alcohol, just drink the orange juice! Use any cheap and cheerful sparkling wine – it's not necessary to trundle out the best champagne.

75 ml	freshly squeezed orange juice	3 fl oz
75 ml	cold sparkling wine	3 fl oz

Pour the orange juice into a wine glass and top up with ice-cold sparkling wine (about half and half).

Lemonade; Real Planters' Punch; Buck's Fizz

Nimboo Pan

Meera Taneja told me that no Indian summer would be complete without this lemon drink.

600 ml	water or mineral water	1 pint
2–3	lemons or limes, juice of	2–3
	crushed ice	
	either sugar or salt and pepper, to taste	

Mix the water and lemon or lime juice, and add the crushed ice. Add either the sugar or the seasoning to taste, and serve with mint.

Citron Pressé
This is the French version of lemonade, as sipped on the boulevards of Paris, and what could be more delicious?

Squeeze a lemon into a glass. Top up with iced water and add sugar to taste.

Classic Cocktails with Jaffa
The method is the same for all: shake, strain, pour and drink.

Daiquiri
1 part lime to 3 parts rum. Add 3 dashes of grenadine.

Orange Blossom
Equal parts gin and orange juice.

Whisky Sour (or Gin Sour or Brandy Sour)
4 parts whisky to 1 part lemon juice, add 5 ml spoon (1 teaspoon) sugar syrup and a dash of orange bitters.

Gin Fizz
Equal parts gin and lemon juice, with icing sugar to taste. Strain and top up with soda water.

Apricot Cooler

Mix the juice of ½ lemon or 1 lime, 2 dashes of grenadine and 1 liqueur glass of apricot brandy. Shake and strain into a tumbler. Fill up with soda water.

Cuba Libre

Mix the juice of ½ lime, 50 ml (2 fl oz) rum, 200 ml (7 fl oz) cola. Combine in a tall glass with a sliver of lime rind and ice.

Jaffa Mull
Makes 6 glasses

Mixing grapefruit and wine might sound odd, but it works very well in this warming winter drink.

2	large grapefruit	2
600 ml	red wine	1 pint
1	stick of cinnamon	1
4	cloves	4
100 g	granulated sugar	4 oz
2 x 15 ml spoon	brandy	2 tablespoons

Squeeze the juice from the fruit and put it in a saucepan. Remove the pips from the pulp left in the squeezer and add this pulp to the pan. Add the wine, cinnamon stick and cloves. Add the sugar and stir over a medium heat until the sugar is dissolved. Bring the mixture almost to the boil and then cover and simmer for 10 minutes (don't let it boil).

Stir in the brandy just before serving and remove the cinnamon stick and cloves if possible. Put spoons in the glasses before pouring in the liquid, to prevent them from cracking, or serve in mugs.

This is even better when made in advance and reheated. When increasing quantities, use only half as much again of the spices.

Use any leftover mull to make a lovely jelly: just add gelatine in the proportions of 15 ml spoon (1 tablespoon) to each 600 ml (1 pint) liquid. (Soften the gelatine in a little cold water and dissolve in the hot mull, then leave to set.)

Trio

Makes 3 glasses.

1	grapefruit, juice and pulp of	1
1	orange, juice and pulp of	1
1	lemon, juice and pulp of	1
150 ml	soda water	¼ pint
4	ice cubes	4
2 x 15 ml spoon	orange liqueur	2 tablespoons

Mix the fruit pulp and juices with the soda water and ice cubes. Add the orange liqueur, mix well and serve immediately.